THE LOW-CARB
BARBECUE BOOK

THE LOW-CARB BARBECUE BOOK

*Over 200 Recipes for
the Grill and Picnic Table*

DANA CARPENDER

FAIR WINDS
PRESS
GLOUCESTER, MASSACHUSETTS

First published in the USA in 2004 by
Fair Winds Press
33 Commercial Street
Gloucester, MA 01930

08 07 06 05 04   2 3 4 5

ISBN 1-59233-055-X

Library of Congress Cataloging-in-Publication Data available

Cover design by Mary Ann Smith
Design by Leslie Haimes

Printed in Canada

This one's for my mom and dad.

contents

Introduction

Barbecue!

It's a word to conjure with, isn't it? Few things can set the mouth to watering like the smell of wood smoke and food grilling in the open air.

What is it about barbecuing and grilling that makes outdoor, open-fire cooking an American obsession? It's the whole wonderful casual ambience, the smells, the sunshine, the laughter. It's the gentle (and sometimes even cutthroat!) rivalry of barbecue contests. It's the fact that the food tastes far better, somehow, than the exact same ingredients would taste cooked indoors.

But I think it's also because we're only a few generations from a frontier society, where cooking was done over an open fire, indoors or out, out of necessity. While the ancient civilizations of Europe were turning out delicate and sophisticated sauces and pastries in well-equipped kitchens, our forefathers and foremothers were cooking over campfires and fireplaces, using every ounce of culinary ingenuity they had to turn what had often been considered poor cuts of meat—spare ribs, brisket, and the like—into a robust and delicious cuisine worthy to stand alongside the greatest cooking in the world.

In many ways, barbecuing and grilling seem ideal for the low-carbohydrate dieter. After all, generous slabs of meat, poultry, or fish—the staples of our diet—are usually featured. But one glance at the label on that bottle of commercial barbecue sauce—or, for that matter, the usual recipes for homemade barbecue sauce—and the pitfalls start coming into focus. Simply put, barbecue sauce is loaded with sugar. A quick glance at my trusty food-count book shows that most brands range between 8 and 14 grams of carbohydrate for a 2-tablespoon serving. Barbecue sauce recipes routinely start with sugary commercial ketchup, and then add a cup or more of sugar!

Add to the sugary sauces the usual barbecue side dishes (or maybe I should call them the usual suspects): potato salad, baked beans, coleslaw with sugary dressing, bowls of chips, onion rings, hush puppies, and lots of beer or soda to wash it down, and that grilled protein is drowned in a flood of carbs!

Yet I know of very few people who can't be seduced by the lure of the grill. Clearly, if we're going to make low carb a lifetime way of eating, we need a way to have our barbecue without losing our waistlines and our health.

And that, my friend, is why I spent the summer of 2003 grilling or barbecuing everything in sight, mixing up rubs, stirring up sauces, and doing my best to come up with lower-carb versions of all our barbecue favorites. I mean, I love barbecue as much as anyone! (And just as well—more mornings than not I ended up eating leftover barbecue for breakfast, for Pete's sake. If I'm going to stick with this cookbook thing, I really need to adopt a half dozen teenaged boys to eat the leftovers . . .)

Here are the results! Barbecue sauces that will blow you away! Marinades that turn tough cuts of meat tender and delicious! Rubs that add irresistible flavor to everything in their path!

And take a look at the side dishes—you'll never miss the potato salad, and there's a pile of new, exciting twists on the same old slaw. There are great grilled vegetables you can cook right alongside your meat, poultry, or fish, and there are new dips that will give you something great to nosh on while the grill masters do their thing. I've even come up with reduced-carb onion rings, hush puppies, and baked beans!

So fire up the grill! It's time for a low-carb barbecue!

chapter one

Techniques and Other Stuff You Need to Know

The Difference Between Grilling and True Barbecue

If you're like me, you've grown up referring to any sort of cooking on an outdoor grill as a "barbecue." Live and learn; we've been wrong all along. Turns out that "barbecue" has a far more specific meaning: slow, indirect cooking by hot smoke, in a closed grill, pit, or smoker. "Grilling" is quicker cooking directly over a fire. Do not confuse the two to a true barbecue fanatic, or you may find yourself whacked upside the head with a rib bone.

This discovery of indirect cooking in a closed grill was a revelation to me. I've always been a good cook, but until I learned the difference between grilling and barbecuing, I couldn't turn out a decent slab of ribs to save my life, and I seriously cremated more than one batch. Now my ribs turn out succulent, smoky, and delicious every time.

Which is not to say that grilling isn't a terrific way of cooking, too, because it certainly is! In this book you'll find both grilling and barbecue recipes. I just wanted to make the difference clear. Now that I've explained it, let's go on to the details of this "indirect cooking by hot smoke" thing, shall we?

Indirect Cooking with Smoke—The True Barbecue

So, how do you do this indirect-smoking thing? Well, if you're a real barbecue fanatic, you buy an actual barbecue pit, designed to do specifically this, and nothing but this. However, if you're a real barbecue fanatic, you certainly don't need any advice or explanation from me—you can skip right to the rubs, mops, and sauces.

Chances are, however, that you don't want to invest in a special piece of equipment for the sole purpose of barbecuing. Panic not; you can do this indirect-smoking thing on your regular grill, be it a charcoal grill or a gas grill, provided that it has a hood. That's really the only feature that is essential: a hood to hold in the heat and smoke. Other than that, you can improvise to fit the equipment at hand.

As I said, "barbecue" specifically refers to food that is not cooked over a fire, but rather is cooked oh-so-slowly by smoke and indirect heat. How slowly? While writing this book I cooked more than one dinner that took nine hours of smoking, and it's not at all uncommon for ribs to take six hours. Barbecue is not a meal for people who need to be out and about all day! It is, however, just fine for a summer Saturday when you plan to be puttering around the house and yard; you can get other things done while tending to your 'cue every half hour to 45 minutes. (On busier days, you can grill things instead—it's much quicker!)

You can perform this incredibly slow-motion cooking process either on a charcoal grill or on a gas grill. It's a toss-up as to which is preferable: charcoal is far more traditional and yields modestly tastier results; gas takes considerably less work and trouble and gives steadier heat. Personally, having done this for a few months, I've settled on gas as my barbecuing fuel of choice, but then no one ever accused me of being a purist. Here's a rundown on how to slow smoke over charcoal or gas.

Chips and Chunks

Whether you're using charcoal or gas, you'll need wood chips or chunks for creating the smoke that flavors the food. You can buy chips and chunks of various kinds anywhere grills are sold, and a fair number of other places, too—I got most of mine at Kmart! There is actually quite a variety of different chips and chunks for sale—most folks have heard of mesquite grilling, but you can also buy apple wood, cherry wood, and all sorts of other chips. One of my favorites is oak chips made from old Jack Daniels barrels—they carry a strong aroma of the bourbon they once held. Experiment to see what you like; I haven't used a wood chip I was really unhappy with yet.

For that matter, if you're getting trees trimmed in your yard, and you have an oak or hickory or apple tree or the like, there's no reason not to chip it up and use it for barbecuing, although chances are you'll need only a tiny fraction of the chips this will create.

Before you even build your fire or turn on your grill, you'll want to start soaking your wood chips or chunks in water—just throw them in any handy container and cover them with water. They'll need to soak a minimum of a half hour before you use them, and longer won't hurt a bit. I just keep a big plastic bowl full of water and chips by my grill most of the time.

Charcoal

First of all, it is imperative that you have a charcoal grill with a hood or lid— an open brazier or hibachi will not do for true barbecue. If your charcoal grill has a thermometer set into the hood, so much the better! Furthermore, for slow smoking you will need a secondary grill for starting new coals in, and fire tongs for transferring them. This secondary grill does not need to have a hood or much of anything else except a fireproof grate where you can start coals burning.

Build a good-sized charcoal fire in your grill, but do not build it in the center of the grill. Build it to one side. Your food will go over on the other side of your grill, see? (Actually, there are numerous opinions on how to do this. Some barbecue geniuses—also called pit masters—want you to build two smaller fires, one on either side of the grill, and put the food in between them. Still others want you to build the fire in the middle, then use tongs to move the hot coals into a ring around the outside of the grill. Others like the build-it-to-one-side method but want you to transfer about a dozen coals to the other side of the grill. Who am I to argue? I just build the fire on one side, put the food on the other side, and I've been getting good results. It's not only easier to build, it's also easier to put the soaked wood chips in one place than in a bunch of places.)

Okay, you've built your charcoal fire, and your meat is seasoned and ready to smoke. Wait for the coals to ash over, at least 15 to 20 minutes. Oil your grill, or spray it with nonstick cooking spray. Caution: If you're using nonstick cooking spray, take the grill off of the fire before spraying, and do not spray in the direction of the fire! The stuff is flammable, and you could get badly burned.

Put a big handful of your soaked wood chips, or two or three soaked wood chunks, on your fire. Put the grill over the fire, and put your meat on the side of the grill where the fire isn't. Close the hood to keep in the smoke!

After your meat has been smoking for about 20 minutes to a half hour, place roughly 15 charcoal briquettes in your secondary grill, and start them burning. When these new coals turn white and ashy all over, transfer them into the main grill with fireproof tongs. Add a new handful of soaked wood chips or another couple of soaked wood chunks, mop your meat (if you're using a mopping sauce), and re-cover the grill. Repeat this process roughly every 45 minutes for however many hours it takes for your 'cue to be done to perfection.

No, really. This is what it takes to keep a charcoal fire going for the extended periods needed to cook true barbecue. The actual logistics of the charcoal transfer will depend on the design of your main grill.

Weber Kettles—the most popular brand of charcoal grill—are designed so that you can slip new coals down onto the fire grate without moving the cooking grill; you just put them through near the handles. This means, of course, that you must situate your grill so that the handle, and the hole, are over your pile of burning charcoal. You can also slip new wood chips through the same way.

However, my charcoal grill does not have this sort of easy access. To add fresh coals and wood chips, I have to take the food off the grill and lift the grill off. This is certainly possible, with a good pair of barbecue gloves and a pot holder, but it's tedious. Indeed, after doing this for nine hours, making Carolina pulled pork, I bought a gas grill!

Warning! Do not do the whole charcoal transferring bit while barefoot. The voice of painful experience here—I dropped one coal, and while I picked it up quickly, I then stepped on a small, glowing chunk that had broken off. Ouch.

Gas

The advantages of gas grills for the sort of long, drawn-out cooking times needed for true barbecue are apparent once you've read the section above. So long as you have propane in your tank, you can maintain a steady temperature. Indeed, the only problem is that you don't get quite the same full-bodied smoky barbecue flavor from a gas grill as you do with charcoal, even with wood chips or chunks. However, you can get quite a good flavor, and to my way of thinking, the greater ease of maintaining the barbecue makes it a worthwhile trade-off. (Serious pit masters, please save your letters of outrage! I happen to know that plenty of competitive barbecue mavens use gas-fired barbecue pits.)

Keep in mind, if you choose gas, that all of your good, smoky barbecue flavor is going to come from the wood chips or chunks you add to the grill. You'll want to check your grill frequently to make sure that whichever you're using is still smoking, and replace your chips or chunks every half hour to 45 minutes.

Other than regularly adding chips or chunks, gas-grill barbecuing is quite simple. Assuming you have a two-burner grill, you light one burner and set it on medium-low heat, add your chips or chunks, and put your meat over the unlit burner. Add more chips or chunks regularly, basting your meat at the same time, and that's it.

Placing the chips or chunks works a little differently on various models of gas grill, the big difference being whether you have the sort of grill that uses lava rock or another sort of heat diffuser, or whether you have one of the new models that don't use any sort of diffuser. Go by the instruction manual that came with your grill for precise instructions, but in general, if you have rock or another diffuser, you can simply put a handful of chips or a couple of wood chunks directly on the rocks. If you, like me, have a no-diffuser grill, you wrap a generous handful of soaked wood chips in foil, and poke a bunch of holes in the packet with a fork or knife. Then you flip over the metal "tent" over the burner that will actually be lit, and place the packet of chips in the cup formed. Make up several packets at a time (this is very easy) and have them sitting by to drop in every time your grill stops smoking. (This involves lifting the grill, I'm afraid.) Other than mopping your barbecue, assuming you're using a mopping sauce, that's all the maintenance you'll have to do.

The Drip Pan

Whichever you're using, charcoal or gas, it's a good idea to place a drip pan under your barbecue, or you'll end up with a big ol' mess. An inexpensive disposable aluminum foil baking pan is perfect, and you can just toss it when it gets too scuzzy. Put this under the grill on the side where you'll be putting your meat.

What about Temperature?

I've found that for my purposes, keeping my grill right around 225°F (110°C) for slow, indirect smoking is just about perfect. I confess, there have been times I've run a grill as low as 180°F (85°C), due to trouble getting a decent fire going (that's how I ended up cooking my pulled pork for nine hours), and there have been times I've checked and found my grill had gotten up to 300°F (150°C). But overall, I aim for a temperature of 225°F. As noted, it's far easier to keep a steady temperature with gas than with charcoal, but practice will help you learn how big a fire you need.

You will want a thermometer to help you keep tabs on grill temperature. As mentioned in the section on tools, if your grill doesn't have a built-in thermometer, a simple oven thermometer, available cheaply in the housewares aisle of every grocery store, Kmart, and Wal-Mart on the planet, will do nicely.

Keep in mind that the weather will make a difference in your grill temperature. Not surprisingly, you'll need a bigger, hotter fire on cold and/or rainy days than on hot sunny ones. Practice makes perfect. And, face it, even when it's not perfect, most barbecue is darned good.

The Last 20 Minutes

As we'll discuss when we get to the section about rubs, mops, sauces, and so forth, you must never, ever, ever put your barbecue sauce—properly called a finishing sauce—on your ribs from the very beginning of the cooking process. Big no-no; that's why it's called a finishing sauce! It has a nasty tendency to burn, you see. Here's what you do:

When your cooking time is almost up, and you've got about 20 minutes left to go, that's when you paint your ribs with finishing sauce. You can also move your 'cue directly over that low, slow fire for the last 20 minutes or so, to crisp it up a bit, if you like.

That being said, I have, on occasion, completely ignored this treatment and simply pulled my unsauced barbecue out of the grill, thrown it on a platter, painted it with sauce, and served it. And it was mighty tasty, too.

The Great Simmering Controversy

Okay, you have a slab of ribs, and you have a craving for barbecue, but you don't have the 5–6 hours it generally takes to smoke a slab from scratch, or maybe you just don't want to take that kind of time. What's a body to do?

Well, some of us simmer that slab of ribs for 25 minutes or so before proceeding to the rub, the mop, and the hot smoke. This simple maneuver cuts the smoking time in half, which is darned impressive if you ask me. It also tends to make the ribs moister, which may or may not be to your liking; I rather enjoy it myself.

However, simmering your ribs before smoking them is heresy to many serious pit masters. So, if you're really, really serious about this stuff, don't simmer, take the time, and you'll turn out ribs that will make the true barbecue buffs smile. But if you're long on desire but short on time, be aware that simmering your ribs can save you up to 3 hours of cooking time. You'll still have to smoke your ribs for a good 2–3 hours, but that's a far cry from 6 hours! And I promise you, your ribs will still taste fantastic.

Simmering, by the way, is certainly preferable to trying to speed up things by smoking your ribs at a higher temperature than you otherwise would. First of all, use a hot fire and your chips or chunks will flare up, instead of smoldering slowly, and there goes your smoke—and your good smoky flavor. Second, you'll get ribs that are dryer and tougher than you'd like.

If you decide you want to simmer your ribs, put them in a really big kettle with just enough water to cover—depending on the size of your kettle, you may want to split your slab into two shorter pieces, to make it fit. I like to throw a tablespoon or two of whatever rub I'll be using into the water. Bring the water to a simmer, and then set your stove timer for 20–25 minutes—meanwhile, get your fire going. When the simmering time is up, pull your ribs out of the water, pat them dry, and proceed with the rub and the smoking.

And for heaven's sake, if you're having a serious competitive barbecue type over for dinner, don't breathe a word about the simmering. Just soak up the compliments.

About Brining

When we started talking seriously about my writing this book, my editor Holly said, "You have to write about brining!" Since I had just recently started brining foods myself, and was impressed with the results, I readily agreed.

"What the heck is brining?" I hear you cry. Brining is the soaking of meat (or poultry or fish) in a seasoned salt-water solution, or brine, for anywhere from a half hour (for shrimp) up to all day or even overnight (for whole pork loins and turkeys and such). Why would you do such a thing? Because when you soak meat in a solution that is saltier than the meat juices, a basic biological force called osmotic pressure causes that salt solution to be drawn into the meat. This accomplishes two things: It seasons the meat internally, not only with salt, but with whatever other seasonings you've added to the brine, and it adds moisture to the meat so that it's wonderfully juicy, even after grilling or slow smoking.

Indeed, the first time I tried brining, I split a rack of ribs in half, brined one half, and didn't brine the other. I then smoked them for the same length of time. While both were very tasty, there was a remarkable difference in the plumpness and juiciness of the ribs that had been brined. I was truly thrilled to find a procedure so simple that had such dramatic—and delicious—results!

The basic proportions for brining that I like to use are about 1/4 cup (60 grams) salt to a quart of water. It's best to use kosher salt or sea salt for brining, because they have no additives—kosher salt is cheaper. You can use table salt in a pinch, but cut the quantity by about 1/4—the smaller grains means it packs tighter in the measuring spoon. You'll want to make enough brine to completely submerge whatever meat you're brining.

How long should you brine things for? It depends on how big your piece of meat is, and how much surface area it has, but the rough rule of thumb is 1–2 hours per pound. Small pieces of food should be brined for shorter periods of time than big hunks of meat—roasts and the like. Shrimp, being, well, shrimpy, can benefit from just 30 minutes of brining; chicken pieces, pork chops, and such are usually brined for a couple of hours. A whole chicken—3–4 pounds—would brine for 8–10 hours, a whole pork loin for about 12 hours, and a whole turkey—12–15 pounds—would brine for 24 hours or so.

Don't leave a piece of meat, poultry, or fish with a brining time of a few hours sitting in the brine for far longer—it will go past juicy to waterlogged. You have an hour or so of leeway, but brining things for twice or three times the proper interval won't give the results you want.

Useful tip: If you have to be out of the house all day, simply brine a larger piece of meat. For instance, Holly (who, of course, spends long hours at the office helping to make me a success, bless her) likes to brine a whole boneless pork loin, leaving it to soak for the 9 or so hours that she's out of the house. When she gets home, she cuts the pork loin into slices about 1" (2.5 centimeters) thick, and has smaller, quick cooking cuts. Very clever!

The Interchangeability Factor

This seems as good a place as any to point out that just because I have used a particular cut of meat, fish, or poultry for a particular recipe doesn't mean you have to do it the same way. Indeed, I'll let you in on a little secret: for any given recipe on any given day, the decision between, say, spare ribs and country-style ribs, or pork steaks versus pork chops, or chicken versus turkey, was made largely on the basis of what I had in the freezer or what was on sale at my grocery store.

Certainly any seasoning that tastes good on pork spare ribs will taste good on country-style pork ribs or on slabs of boneless pork loin. For that matter, most seasonings that taste good on pork also taste good on chicken. And certainly anything I've done with one sort of poultry you can do with another—for instance, feel free to use a marinade or brine I've used on chicken to season turkey legs or a turkey breast. Bastes used on whole salmon can be used on salmon steaks or fillets, and vice versa.

In short, play around!

On the Inherently Inaccurate Nature of This Book

I must confess, I really looked forward to writing this book—until I started to write it. From the beginning, the food was wonderful, but I didn't realize until I really got into it the difficulties that this sort of book presents, especially in a format where accurate nutritional statistics are a lot of what the reader is paying for, and when a lot of my readership looks to me to give clear instructions on how to prepare a dish.

It is nearly impossible to be really precise and accurate with these recipes, and that fact almost drove me out of my mind (not that far to go, admittedly). Why is it impossible to be accurate?

The Grill

First of all, these outdoor methods of cooking—grilling and indirect-heat smoking—are nowhere near as predictable as working with a stove in the controlled environment of a kitchen. Are you using a gas grill or a charcoal grill? Right there, we're talking a sizable difference in control.

But it's even flukier than that! Are you using a gas grill that has a bed of lava rock to spread heat, or one of the new ones that claim not to need heat diffusion? If you're using a charcoal grill, how good are you at building a hot, lasting fire? I, by way of example, know that I can't build a good, hot charcoal fire as well as my Eagle Scout husband can—and how good you are at building a fire can make a considerable difference in cooking times.

Once you've got your fire, be it gas or charcoal, how close to the flame is your grill? Can your grill be moved up and down? How about your fire grate?

You can see that this is a flukier process than setting an oven to a particular temperature and leaving the food in it for a set number of minutes! I will do my best to describe cooking temperatures and times, but please be aware that they are all approximate. There is no substitute for paying attention to your own grill and to your food—and for the judicious use of a meat thermometer and an oven thermometer, or the thermometer built into the hood of your grill.

The Nutritional Calculations

Unlike my previous cookbooks, you'll find that there are a lot of recipes in this book where the carb counts are admittedly approximate. Why? Because we will be marinating things and basting things—and in either case, we will almost never consume all of the marinade or basting sauce (often called mopping sauce). It is simply impossible for me to predict exactly how much of the marinade or baste you will use.

I've decided to handle the problem this way: I will tell you how many grams of carbohydrate are in the whole recipe, including all of the marinade, baste, or mopping sauce, and then I will approximate, from how much I have ended up using, what a reasonable figure is for the finished dish, per serving. Better than this I cannot do, I'm afraid, unless someone would like to give me a sizable grant to pay for scientific analysis of every dish—and that still wouldn't tell us how many carbs *your* dish will come out with!

Why Aren't There Calorie Counts in This Book?

Many of you asked me to include calorie counts in this book. But because of the nature of barbecue cooking, it is impossible to accurately measure the calorie counts because there is no way of knowing exactly how much of the marinade you will consume.

Useful Barbecuing Tools

Here, in no particular order, are the tools that will make your barbecuing and grilling easier and more successful:

- **Long-handled basting brush**—Use this to spread mopping sauce and finishing sauce.

- **Tongs**—These are for handling your food. Long-handled tongs are best, but I've used my regular kitchen tongs quite a lot, with no problem. It is best to handle your 'cue with tongs; sticking a fork in it will let out juice.

- **Fire tongs**—If you're doing your smoking with a charcoal fire, you'll need a pair of fireproof tongs dedicated to moving coals from your secondary grill into the main grill. Mine are iron and get a good, secure grip on a single briquette. These also are helpful for lifting the hot grill so you can put more chips or chunks on the fire.

- **Barbecue gloves**—These are long, heavy rubber gloves, and mine have a flannel lining. Barbecue gloves let you handle meat on the grill without burning your hands, and without the mess that would ensue if you used a regular cloth hot mitt. These are particularly useful when you're barbecuing something too bulky to pick up with tongs—a whole chicken, a pork shoulder, a whole on-the-bone turkey breast, or anything else that's big! You should be able to find barbecue gloves at stores that carry a big selection of grills and other barbecuing equipment.

- **Oven thermometer**—If your grill didn't come with a built-in thermometer, pick up one in the housewares aisle of your grocery store. It is indispensable for learning what settings on your gas grill deliver what level of heat, or learning to gauge how big a fire to build in your charcoal grill.

- **Timer**—If you're outside the house, you can't exactly be using the oven timer, now can you? Pick up a cheap timer in the housewares aisle to use while grilling. You'll cremate less chicken that way. (Remember to bring it back inside when you're done; rain does electronic timers no good at all.)

- **Meat thermometer**—Using one is the only way to know for sure if your barbecue is done through. The standard sort is great for large items—pork shoulder and whole chickens and such—but the instant-read type is very useful for things like burgers and ribs.

- **Meat injector**—This is a cool device that lets you inject marinades right into your food. As you might suspect, a meat injector looks like a big, scary hypodermic syringe. Since you're using it to doctor your meat, I suppose that's fitting. Available at housewares stores.

- **Spatula or pancake turner**—This is obviously the tool of choice for flipping burgers and the like. You may want one with a long handle!

- **Squirt bottle**—When fat drips off of your food into the fire during grilling, you'll get flare-ups. It's essential that you have a squirt bottle of water on hand to squirt on the coals to fight off those flare-ups, or you'll end up with blackened food, and we ain't talking Cajun cuisine.

- **Small-holed grill rack**—If you want to grill things that are small enough to fall through your grill—asparagus, sliced onions, shrimp, whatever—a small-holed grill rack is what you need. It's just another grate but with smaller holes—duh! It will be either a wire grid or a solid piece of metal pierced with holes. Find a small-holed grill rack wherever grills are sold.

- **Grill wok**—This is a very cool item. It's a square, slope-sided metal basket with holes all over. You set the grill wok on your grill over a good hot fire, put in your food—veggies, seafood, what have you—and stir "fry" it until done. Not as common as small-holed grill racks, but look at a store that has a good, complete grill-and-barbecue section, and you'll probably find one. (I got mine at TJ Maxx!)

- **Nonreactive bowls and pans**—We do a lot of marinating in this book, and if you marinate in aluminum, iron, copper, or some other material that reacts with the often acidic ingredients we use, you'll end up with odd results. You need containers that are nonreactive: glass, stainless steel, anodized aluminum, enamel, plastic. You'll also want to use nonreactive pans for cooking barbecue sauces—standard stainless steel saucepans are fine—because virtually all barbecue sauces are acidic.

Ingredients

Most of the ingredients in this book will be very familiar, but there are a few that you may not have encountered before. Here's a quick rundown:

- **Atkins Bake Mix and Atkins Cornbread Mix**—There are just two recipes in this book that call for these products, but they're awfully good recipes. If stores in your area aren't carrying Atkins products yet, you can easily get these from a whole raft of low-carbohydrate e-tailers (retail Web sites).

- **Avocados**—Several recipes in this book call for avocados. Be aware that the little, black, rough-skinned avocados are far lower in carbohydrates (and higher in healthy monounsaturated fat) than the big green ones are. All nutritional analyses were done assuming you are using little black avocados.

- **Beer**—A few recipes in this book call for beer. The lowest-carbohydrate beers on the market at this writing are Michelob Ultra, at 2.8 grams per bottle, and Miller Lite and Milwaukee's Best Light, both 3.5 grams per can. These are what I recommend you use. They are also what I recommend you drink, if you're a beer fan.

- **Blackstrap molasses**—What the heck is molasses doing in a low-carb cookbook?! It's practically all carbohydrate, after all. Well, yes, but I've found that combining Splenda with a small amount of molasses gives a good brown-sugar flavor to all sorts of recipes—and many, many barbecue sauce and rub recipes call for brown sugar! Always use the darkest molasses you can find—the darker it is, the stronger the flavor and the lower the carb count. That's why I specify blackstrap, the darkest, strongest molasses there is. It's nice to know that blackstrap is also where all the minerals they take out of sugar end up—it may be carb-y, but at least it's not a nutritional wasteland. Still, I use only small amounts.

Why not use some of the artificial brown sugar–flavored sweeteners out there? Because I've tried them, and I haven't tasted one I would be willing to buy again. Ick.

- **Chili garlic paste**—This is actually a traditional Asian ingredient, consisting mostly, as the name strongly implies, of hot chilies and garlic. This seasoning saves lots of time when we want a recipe to be both hotly spicy and garlicky. Chili garlic paste comes in jars and keeps for months in the refrigerator. Worth seeking out at Asian markets or particularly complete grocery stores.

- **Diet-Rite tangerine soda**—Just a few recipes in this book call for Diet-Rite tangerine soda. I've specified Diet-Rite brand because it's sweetened with sucralose (Splenda) rather than with aspartame. This is important because aspartame loses its sweetness when heated for any length of time, while sucralose does not. Diet-Rite is nationally distributed, I understand, so you should be able to find it. If you can find another brand of tangerine- or orange-flavored diet soda that is sweetened with sucralose instead of aspartame, feel free to substitute it (and let me know!). However, do not substitute aspartame-sweetened soda. Your recipe won't come out right.

- **Fish sauce** (nuoc mam or nam pla)—This is a salty, fermented seasoning widely used in Southeast Asian cooking. It is available in Asian grocery stores and in the Asian food section of big grocery stores. Grab it when you find it; it keeps nicely without refrigeration. Fish sauce is used in a few (really great) recipes in this book, and adds an authentic flavor. In a pinch, you can substitute soy sauce, although you'll lose some of your Southeast Asian accent.

- **Fruit$_2$O**—Say "fruit two-oh," as in H$_2$O with fruit flavor added. Fruit$_2$O is a new, nationally distributed beverage line consisting of water with natural fruit flavors and a touch of Splenda. It's a wonderful, refreshing thing to drink. More important for our purposes here, however, is the fact that it lets us add fruit flavors to recipes without adding carbohydrates or calories. You'll find a few recipes calling for peach-flavored, lemon-flavored, and orange-flavored Fruit$_2$O in this book. Look for Fruit$_2$O in the water aisle of your grocery store.

- **Guar and xanthan gums**—These sound just dreadful, don't they? But they're in lots of your favorite processed foods, so how bad can they be? What the heck are they? They're forms of water-soluble fiber, extracted and purified. Guar and xanthan are both flavorless white powders; their value to us is as low-carb thickeners. Technically speaking, these are carbs, but they're all fiber. Nothing but. So don't worry about it.

Your health food store may well be able to order guar or xanthan for you—I slightly prefer xanthan, myself—if they don't have it on hand. You can also find suppliers online. Keep either one in a jar with a tight lid, and it will never go bad—I bought a pound of guar about fifteen years ago and it's still going strong!

- **Low-sugar preserves**—I've used low-sugar apricot preserves and low-sugar orange marmalade in a few recipes in this book. I buy Smucker's brand, and like it very much. This is lower in sugar by far than the "all fruit" preserves, which replace sugar with concentrated fruit juice. Folks, sugar from fruit juice is still sugar.

Smucker's also makes artificially sweetened preserves, but they're only about 1 gram less carbohydrate per serving than the low-sugar preserves, since they still have the sugar from the fruit, and many people prefer to avoid aspartame, so I use the low-sugar variety.

- **Polyol sweeteners**—Also called sugar alcohols, the polyols are the sweeteners of choice for most commercially made sugar-free sweets. These sweeteners are carbohydrates, but they're carbohydrates made of molecules so large it's difficult for your body to digest or absorb them. For a long time, these sweeteners were not available for home use, but since low-carb dieting has become so popular, they're starting to pop up in stores that carry low-carb specialty products, and most particularly on the low-carb e-tail Web sites. I actually have three varieties of polyols in my kitchen as I write this: isomalt, erythritol, and maltitol. (Most polyols have names that end in "-tol"; I don't know what happened to isomalt.)

I've used polyols in some recipes to get a bit of that syrupy quality that barbecue sauces and glazes generally have. However, if you can't get polyol sweeteners, find them too expensive (they are steep!), or prefer not to use them, you can substitute an equal quantity of granular Splenda.

The one big exception to this rule is the dessert recipes. Some sort of polyol sweetener is essential for making the sugar-free chocolate sauce in the dessert chapter; Splenda simply will not work. Furthermore, not even all polyols work! I found that the chocolate sauce works beautifully with maltitol, but when I made it with erythritol, it turned grainy as it cooled. I didn't get a chance to try it with isomalt or any of the other polyols.

If you can't find polyol sweeteners in your hometown, check the appendix at the back of the book for online sources.

One important thing to remember about polyols: Like all indigestible carbohydrates, these will cause gas and diarrhea if eaten in quantity—and the definition of "quantity" varies from person to person.

- **Rice protein powder**—Only one recipe in this book calls for rice protein powder, although there are also recipes in my other cookbooks that use it. I buy Nutribiotic brand of rice protein, which has 1 gram of carbohydrate per tablespoon, but any unflavored rice protein powder with a similar carb count should work fine. If you can't find rice protein powder, ask your local health food store to order it for you—most health food stores are lovely about special orders. I'm guessing that any unflavored protein powder you have on hand would be an okay substitute, but since I haven't tested them all, that's just a guess.

- **Splenda**—Splenda is the latest artificial sweetener to hit the market, and it blows all of the competition clear out of the water! Feed nondieting friends and family Splenda-sweetened desserts and they will never know that you didn't use sugar. It tastes that good.

Splenda has some other advantages. The table sweetener has been bulked so that it measures spoon for spoon, cup for cup, like sugar. This makes adapting recipes much easier. Also, Splenda stands up to heat, unlike aspartame, which means you can use it for baked goods and other things that are heated for a while.

However, Splenda is not completely carb-free. Because of the maltodextrin used to bulk it, Splenda has about a 1/2 gram of carbohydrate per teaspoon, or about 1/8 of the carbohydrate of sugar. So count 1/2 gram per teaspoon, 1 1/2 grams per tablespoon, and 24 grams per cup.

It's important to know that the Splenda that comes in little packets measures differently than the Splenda that comes in bulk in boxes (and recently, in a Mylar "Baker's Bag"—this is the cheapest format). It's considerably sweeter. All of these recipes were standardized on bulk Splenda, not the stuff in packets. If all you have on hand is the packets (or if that's all your grocery store carries), the nice folks at the Splenda helpline tell me that 24 packets equal 1 cup (225 grams) of sugar—or of granular Splenda—in sweetness. You can adjust from there.

If you like, you can get Splenda in a carb-free liquid form, but you'll have to order it. You'll also have to work out on your own how much to use; I used the widely available granular Splenda in developing these recipes. For sources of liquid Splenda, see the appendix.

- **Sugar-free imitation honey**—This is one of those "I knew low carb had really hit the mainstream when …" products. I knew we were mainstream when my grocery store started carrying sugar-free imitation honey! This is a polyol syrup with flavoring added to make it taste like honey, and the one I've tried, by HoneyTree, is not a bad imitation. There's another by a company called Steel's. Since many barbecue sauces and glazes call for honey, sugar-free imitation honey is a welcome addition to my kitchen. Check the appendix at the back of the book for online sources.

- **Sugar-free pancake syrup**—Made from polyols, this has the same texture and maple flavor as standard pancake syrup, and lets us add a maple flavor to several dishes. Find sugar-free pancake syrup in any large grocery store, usually with the regular pancake syrup, but sometimes in the "diet" section. The carb count varies some, even discounting the polyols, so that's something to keep in mind. I used Log Cabin brand sugar-free syrup in developing these recipes.

- **Vege-Sal**—If you've read my newsletter, *Lowcarbezine!* you know that I'm a big fan of Vege-Sal. What is Vege-Sal? It's a salt that's been seasoned, but don't think "seasoned salt." Vege-Sal is much milder than traditional seasoned salt. It's simply salt that's been blended with some dried, powdered vegetables; the flavor is quite subtle, but I think it improves all sorts of things. I've given you the choice between using regular salt or Vege-Sal in some of these recipes. Don't worry, they'll come out fine with plain old salt, but I do think Vege-Sal adds a little something extra. Vege-Sal is also excellent sprinkled over chops and steaks, in place of regular salt. Vege-Sal is made by Modern Products and is widely available in health food stores.

chapter two

Sauces, Rubs, Mops, and the Like

Let's talk for a moment about sauces, rubs, and mops because where true smoked barbecue is concerned, this is where it's at. Indeed, the motto of my favorite barbecue joint of all time—Hecky's, in Evanston, Illinois—is "It's the sauce!" And it is the sauce—and the rub, and the mop, so let's get the three straight.

Finishing Sauce

That sweet, spicy, tomatoey stuff you know as "barbecue sauce" is properly referred to as a finishing sauce. It's called a finishing sauce because you don't put it on until your barbecue is almost finished cooking—indeed, some pit masters slap it on right before bearing the fruits of their labors forth to the table. It is a serious mistake to put your finishing sauce on too soon, because it will burn on you, and leave your 'cue with a nasty layer of black carbon instead of the tantalizing spicy-sweetness we all know and love. Paint your barbecue with the finishing sauce of your choice about 20 minutes before your cooking time is up, at most. Then if you'd like to glaze it a little, you can move your 'cue over the fire for 5–10 minutes per side, no more.

Finishing sauces traditionally have a lot of sugar in them. These sauces don't, of course, but since they contain things like tomato paste and low-carb ketchup, they do have some carbs; there's simply no way to make a carb-free barbecue sauce that tastes like barbecue sauce. Still, the highest carb of these sauces has roughly half the carbs of the popular bottled sauces, which ain't bad—and many are considerably lower carb than that.

Rub

A rub is a dry spice mixture that you sprinkle or rub liberally all over the meat to be smoked before you ever put it on the grill. A good rub is a thing of beauty and almost makes a finishing sauce unnecessary. Indeed, if you're on Induction, or simply trying to get the most flavor for the very fewest carbs, consider using a good rub and skipping the finishing sauce. You can also sprinkle on rubs at the table for extra seasoning, if you like.

Mopping Sauce

Also known simply as a mop. This is a sauce used to baste the meat during the long, slow smoking process, to keep it moist and succulent. The basic proportions of a mop are roughly 50-50—half water, or another watery ingredient like beer or broth, and half oil. Spices and other flavorings are added so that every time you mop your barbecue, it just gets better and better.

It's always good to let your barbecue smoke for about 30 minutes before you start to mop it, to let the rub really get a hold of the meat; otherwise you can mop it right off.

There are several recipes for mops in this chapter and elsewhere in the book, but concocting a simple yet very satisfactory mop is easy: combine 1/2 cup of water, broth, or the like; 1/2 cup of oil; and 1–2 tablespoons of whatever rub you're using, and you'll have a great mop that will keep your meat moist and add plenty of flavor.

I thought about dividing this chapter up, putting the finishing sauces in one section, the rubs in another, and the mops in a third, but there are many "sets" here—rubs, mops, and finishing sauces meant to go together. So, I didn't.

By the way, most barbecue books give you recipes for sauces and rubs that make vast, huge quantities—3 cups of rub or 2 quarts of sauce or whatever. I don't want that much of any of these things hanging around my house, and I figured you don't either, so I kept my quantities smaller. But please, feel free to double, triple, even quadruple any of these recipes.

Dana's No-Sugar Ketchup

This recipe has already appeared in my first two cookbooks, but ketchup is an essential ingredient in many barbecue sauce recipes, so it only made sense to repeat it yet again here. If you're making lots of barbecue sauce, you may as well double this.

6 ounces (170 grams) tomato paste

2/3 cup (160 milliliters) cider vinegar

1/3 cup (80 milliliters) water

1/3 cup (80 milliliters) Splenda

2 tablespoons minced onion

2 cloves garlic

1 teaspoon salt

1/8 teaspoon ground allspice

1/8 teaspoon ground cloves

1/8 teaspoon pepper

Put everything in your blender, and run it until the onion disappears. Scrape into a container with a tight lid, and store in the refrigerator.

YIELD: Makes roughly 1 1/2 cups, or 12 servings of 2 tablespoons apiece

5 grams of carbohydrate per serving, with 1 gram of fiber, for a usable carb count of 4 grams; 1 gram of protein.

☀ Classic Barbecue Rub

As the name suggests, this is rub that cries "classic barbecue"! A great combo with the Kansas City Barbecue Sauce, which follows, but use it with any sauce—and on any meat!

  1/4 cup (60 milliliters) Splenda

  1 tablespoon seasoned salt

  1 tablespoon garlic powder

  1 tablespoon celery salt

  1 tablespoon onion powder

  2 tablespoons paprika

  1 tablespoon chili powder

  2 teaspoons pepper

  1 teaspoon lemon pepper

  1 teaspoon sage

  1 teaspoon dry mustard

  1/2 teaspoon dried thyme

  1/2 teaspoon cayenne

Combine everything, stir well, and store in a shaker. Sprinkle heavily over just about anything, but especially over pork ribs and chicken.

YIELD: Makes just over 2/3 cup, or roughly 12 tablespoons

3 grams of carbohydrate with 1 gram of fiber, for a usable carb count of 2 grams; 1 gram protein.

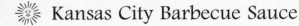 # Kansas City Barbecue Sauce

This is it—what most of us have in mind when we think of barbecue sauce: tomatoey, spicy, and sweet. Unbelievably close to a top-flight commercial barbecue sauce—and my Kansas City–raised husband agrees. If you like a smoky note in your barbecue sauce, add 1 teaspoon of liquid smoke flavoring to this.

>   2 tablespoons butter
>
>   1 clove garlic
>
>   1/4 cup (40 grams) chopped onion
>
>   1 tablespoon lemon juice
>
>   1 cup (240 grams) Dana's No-Sugar Ketchup (page 30)
>
>   1/3 cup (80 milliliters) Splenda
>
>   1 tablespoon blackstrap molasses
>
>   2 tablespoons Worcestershire sauce
>
>   1 tablespoon chili powder
>
>   1 tablespoon white vinegar
>
>   1 teaspoon pepper
>
>   1/4 teaspoon salt

Just combine everything in a saucepan over low heat. Heat until the butter melts, stir the whole thing up, and let it simmer for 5 to 10 minutes. That's it!

YIELD: Roughly 1 3/4 cups, or 14 servings of 2 tablespoons each

Each serving will have 7 grams of carbohydrate, with 1 gram of fiber, for a usable carb count of 6 grams; 1 gram protein.

☼ Cranberry Barbecue Sauce

The cranberries make this a natural with poultry, but it's good with pork, too.

   1/2 cup (120 grams) Dana's No-Sugar Ketchup (page 30)

   1 tablespoon cider vinegar

   1 tablespoon spicy brown mustard

   1 tablespoon Worcestershire sauce

   3 tablespoons Splenda

   1 clove garlic

   1/4 small onion, cut in hunks

   1/4 cup (25 grams) fresh cranberries

   1 dash salt

   1 dash pepper

This one starts in your food processor. Dump everything into the food processor with the S-blade in place, and puree until the cranberries disappear.

Scrape out of the food processor, into a saucepan, and bring to a simmer over low heat. Let it simmer, stirring now and then, for just a few minutes. Thin with a little water if needed.

YIELD: About 1 cup, or 8 servings of 2 tablespoons each

4 grams of carbohydrate, with 1 gram of fiber, for a usable carb count of 3 grams; a trace of protein.

☀ Herb Chicken Rub

This rub has the herbs we traditionally associate with poultry—sage, thyme, and the like. Consider seasoning a chicken with this rub and the matching mop, and then using one of the fruity barbecue sauces—the Cranberry Barbecue Sauce (page 33) or the Apricot White Wine Sauce (page 65), perhaps.

> 1 1/2 teaspoons poultry seasoning
>
> 1 1/2 teaspoons garlic salt
>
> 1 teaspoon dry mustard
>
> 1 teaspoon ground ginger
>
> 1 teaspoon Splenda

Just measure everything into a small dish, and stir it together.

YIELD: Enough rub for 1 good-sized chicken

The whole batch has just 1 gram of carbohydrate, with a trace of fiber.

☀ Herb Chicken Mop

For use with the Herb Chicken Rub, of course!

> 1 teaspoon Herb Chicken Rub (above)
>
> 1/4 cup (60 milliliters) olive oil
>
> 1/4 cup (60 milliliters) chicken broth

Just combine everything, and use to baste chicken during indirect cooking.

YIELD: Makes about 1/2 cup

The whole batch has only a trace of carbohydrate, and you won't use it all up mopping your chicken. Call this one free.

Memphis Rub

    3 tablespoons paprika

    1 tablespoon seasoned salt

    1 tablespoon pepper

    1 1/2 teaspoons garlic powder

    1 1/2 teaspoons cayenne

    1 1/2 teaspoons dried oregano

    1 1/2 teaspoons dry mustard

    1 1/2 teaspoons chili powder

Just mix everything together, and use on ribs, pork chops, or even chicken. Mop with the Memphis Mop (page 37), and finish with one of the Memphis-style sauces!

YIELD: Makes 7 1/2 tablespoons, or about 7 servings

4 grams of carb per serving, with 1 gram of fiber, for a usable carb count of 3 grams; 1 gram protein.

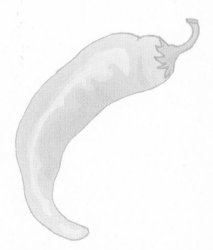

☀ Memphis "Dry Sauce"

Really a rub, but the recipe I adapted this from called it a dry sauce, so who am I to argue?

   1/2 cup (120 milliliters) Splenda
   1/2 teaspoon blackstrap molasses
   1 tablespoon chili powder
   1 tablespoon black pepper
   1 tablespoon dry mustard
   3 teaspoons garlic powder
   1 tablespoon paprika
   1 teaspoon celery salt
   1 teaspoon onion powder

Just combine everything in a food processor or blender until the molasses is distributed—for some odd reason, I find a blender works better for this. Then sprinkle over pork or chicken before smoking.

YIELD: Makes roughly 2/3 of a cup, or 12 servings of 1 tablespoon each

3 grams of carbohydrate and 1 gram of fiber, for a usable carb count of 2 grams; a trace of protein.

⁂ Memphis Mop

This is one of the most complex mopping sauces in this book, and just looking at the ingredients, you can see it's going to add loads of flavor to your 'cue!

1 cup (225 milliliters) water

2 tablespoons Splenda

1/2 teaspoon blackstrap molasses

1 cup (225 milliliters) wine vinegar

2 tablespoons Worcestershire sauce

1/2 teaspoon chili powder

1/2 teaspoon Tabasco sauce

2 tablespoons canola oil

1 clove garlic

Just whisk everything together in a nonreactive bowl or pan and mop away!

YIELD: Makes roughly 2 1/4 cups

7 grams of carbohydrate in the whole batch, which you won't use up even if you do 2 slabs of ribs. We're talking well under 1 extra gram of carbohydrate per serving.

Memphis Sweet Sauce

The obvious choice for ribs seasoned with Memphis Rub (page 35) and mopped with the Memphis Mop (page 37)! It's the mustard that makes this a Memphis-style sauce.

1 tablespoon tomato paste

3 tablespoons water

1/4 cup (60 grams) Dana's No-Sugar Ketchup (page 30)

2 tablespoons spicy brown mustard

1 tablespoon Worcestershire sauce

1 tablespoon butter

1/2 teaspoon lemon juice

1 tablespoon Splenda

1/4 teaspoon blackstrap molasses

1 teaspoon paprika

1 teaspoon seasoned salt

1 clove garlic

Measure everything into a nonreactive saucepan, and whisk it together. Bring to a simmer over low heat, and simmer for 5 minutes or so.

YIELD: Makes roughly 1 cup, or 8 servings of 2 tablespoons each

4 grams of carbohydrate per serving, with 1 gram of fiber, for a usable carb count of 3 grams; 1 gram protein.

☀ Memphis Mustard Barbecue Sauce

This tasty Memphis-style barbecue sauce is one of the lowest-carb sauces in this book, and packs a serious mustard note. Enjoy!

- 1/2 cup (120 milliliters) white vinegar
- 1/4 cup (60 grams) yellow mustard
- 2 tablespoons minced onion
- 1/2 tablespoon paprika
- 2 tablespoons tomato paste
- 2 cloves garlic
- 1/4 teaspoon cayenne
- 1/4 teaspoon pepper
- 1/4 teaspoon salt
- 2 teaspoons Splenda

Just measure everything into a nonreactive saucepan, whisk it together, bring it to a simmer, and let it simmer for 5 minutes or so. That's it!

YIELD: Makes about 1 cup, or 8 servings of 2 tablespoons each

3 grams of carbohydrate each, with 1 gram of fiber, for a usable carb count of just 2 grams; 1 gram protein.

Piedmont Mustard Sauce

This bright-yellow sauce, heavy on the mustard but with no tomato at all, is typical of the Piedmont region of North Carolina. Typically used on pulled pork, but it would be good on any barbecued pork, I think.

- 1/2 cup (120 grams) yellow mustard
- 2 tablespoons lemon juice
- 2 tablespoons Splenda
- 1 tablespoon white vinegar
- 1/4 teaspoon cayenne

Just combine everything in a saucepan, and simmer for 5 minutes over low heat.

YIELD: Makes roughly 3/4 cup, or 6 servings of 2 tablespoons each

2 grams of carbohydrate per serving, with 1 gram of fiber, for a usable carb count of just 1 gram; 1 gram of protein.

❋ Eastern Carolina Vinegar Sauce

This is the traditional eastern Carolina sauce for pulled pork. I'd never had anything like this before researching this book, but it's delicious! It's just sweetened vinegar with a good hit of hot pepper. Try it!

   1/2 cup (120 milliliters) cider vinegar

   1 1/2 tablespoons Splenda

   1/4 teaspoon blackstrap molasses

   1 teaspoon red pepper flakes

   1/4 teaspoon cayenne

Combine all ingredients and stir together.

YIELD: 6 servings

2 grams of carbohydrate and a trace of fiber, for a usable carb count of 2 grams; a trace of protein.

☀ Lexington-Style Barbecue Sauce

This is your third choice for what to mix into your Carolina pulled pork—
mostly vinegary, but with a tomato note.

  1 cup (225 milliliters) cider vinegar

  3/4 cup (180 grams) Dana's No-Sugar Ketchup (page 30)

  3 tablespoons Splenda

  1/2 teaspoon salt

  1/2 teaspoon red pepper flakes

  1/8 teaspoon cayenne

Combine everything in a nonreactive saucepan over low heat, and stir together
well. Bring to a simmer, and let it cook for 15 minutes or so. That's it!

YIELD: Makes roughly 1 3/4 cups, or 14 servings of 2 tablespoons each

6 grams of carbohydrate with 1 gram of fiber, for a usable carb count of 5 grams;
1 gram protein.

☀ Alabama White Sauce

This is unlike any other kind of barbecue sauce—it's mayonnaise based, and when you baste chicken with it during smoking, it creates an amber color and a mellow flavor.

> 1/2 cup (120 grams) mayonnaise
>
> 3 tablespoons white wine vinegar
>
> 1 teaspoon spicy brown mustard
>
> 1/2 teaspoon Creole seasoning (look for this in the spice aisle)
>
> 1 clove garlic, crushed
>
> 1 teaspoon prepared horseradish

Just whisk everything together, and use to baste chicken or as a finishing sauce. However, unlike with many other sauces, you won't want to boil this sauce to kill raw chicken germs—it would ruin the texture of the sauce—so set part of the sauce aside to use as a finishing sauce before you use the rest for basting.

YIELD: Makes about 2/3 cup, or 6 servings of 2 tablespoons each

1 gram of carbohydrate, a trace of fiber, and a trace of protein.

☼ Polynesian Sauce

If a luau is what you're dreaming of, try this sauce! Great on pork of any kind.

> 1/4 cup (65 grams) tomato paste
>
> 1/4 cup (60 milliliters) canned crushed pineapple in juice
>
> 1/4 cup (60 milliliters) white vinegar
>
> 1 tablespoon soy sauce
>
> 2 tablespoons Splenda
>
> 5 tablespoons water
>
> 1/4 teaspoon blackstrap molasses

Combine everything in a saucepan, and simmer over low heat for 5 minutes.

YIELD: Makes a little over 1 cup, or 8 servings of 2 slightly generous tablespoons each

5 grams of carbohydrate per serving, with 1 gram of fiber, for a usable carb count of 4 grams; 1 gram of protein.

 # Big Bad Beef Rib Rub

Oh, boy, oh, boy. I'd never had beef ribs before I made them with this rub, and I was an instant convert!

- 2 tablespoons Splenda
- 2 tablespoons DiabetiSweet or other polyol sweetener
- 2 tablespoons garlic salt
- 2 tablespoons garlic powder
- 2 tablespoons paprika
- 2 teaspoons chili powder
- 1/2 teaspoon ground ginger
- 1/2 teaspoon onion powder
- 1/2 teaspoon ground coriander
- 1/2 teaspoon cayenne

This is extremely simple: Just put everything in a bowl, and stir it together. Sprinkle generously over beef ribs before barbecuing.

YIELD: Roughly 3/4 cup, or 12 tablespoons

Each tablespoonful will have 3 grams of carbohydrate, exclusive of polyols, and 1 gram of fiber, for a usable carb count of 2 grams; 1 gram protein.

Bodacious Beef Brisket Rub

4 tablespoons paprika

1 tablespoon pepper

2 tablespoons Splenda

2 teaspoons chili powder

2 teaspoons onion powder

2 teaspoons garlic powder

1/2 teaspoon cayenne (optional, if you like your food really fiery—but this has plenty of heat without it)

Stir everything together. Save a tablespoon for the mop, and use the rest to sprinkle liberally over your brined brisket.

YIELD: Makes about 8 servings of 1 tablespoon each

4 grams of carbohydrate, 1 gram of fiber, 1 gram protein.

Bodacious Beef Brisket Beer Mop

1 12-ounce (360-milliliter) can or bottle light beer (Michelob Ultra, Miller Lite, or Milwaukee's Best Light are the lowest carb—and Milwaukee's Best Light is the cheapest!)

1/2 cup (120 milliliters) cider vinegar

1/4 cup (60 milliliters) olive oil

2 cloves garlic, crushed

1/4 onion, minced

1 tablespoon Worcestershire sauce

1 tablespoon Bodacious Beef Brisket Rub

Stir everything together, and use to mop your brisket while it's smoking.

YIELD: Makes enough to mop 1-2 briskets (but rarely will you use up the entire batch in the course of cooking).

14 grams of carbohydrate, 1 gram of fiber (in entire batch). But since you won't use the entire batch, and a 4-pound brisket will serve at least 8 people, no one will get more than a couple of grams of carbohydrate.

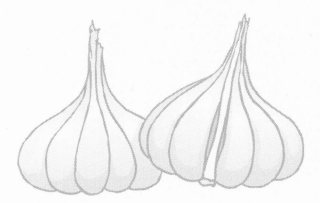

Lone Star Beef Sauce

Forget your pork! In Texas, barbecue means beef, and lots of it. The typical barbecue cut for Texans is brisket, but I like this sauce on beef ribs. Especially if they've been rubbed with the Big Bad Beef Rib Rub (page 45)!

   1 cup (240 grams) Dana's No-Sugar Ketchup (page 30)

   2 tablespoons white vinegar

   2 tablespoons oil

   1 1/2 teaspoons blackstrap molasses

   1 tablespoon sugar-free imitation honey

   2 tablespoons Splenda

   1 1/2 teaspoons Worcestershire sauce

   1 1/2 teaspoons lemon juice

   1 teaspoon pepper

   1 clove garlic

   1/4 teaspoon cayenne

Stir everything together in a saucepan, and let it simmer over low heat for five minutes or so.

YIELD: Makes roughly 1 1/2 cups, or 12 servings of 2 tablespoons each

6 grams of carbohydrate per serving, with 1 gram of fiber, for a usable carb count of 5 grams; 1 gram of protein.

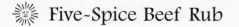 # Five-Spice Beef Rub

Wow! Sort of sweet and Chinese-y. I invented this for beef ribs, but there's no law that says you can't use it on brisket or even on a steak.

    2 tablespoons five-spice powder

    2 tablespoons garlic salt

    1 tablespoon Splenda

Simply combine everything and stir well. Sprinkle over beef ribs before barbecuing—but set aside 1 1/2 teaspoons of the rub first, to make the Five-Spice Beef Mop (page 50).

YIELD: Makes 5 tablespoons (but then, you'd figured that out already, right?)

Each tablespoonful will have 2 grams of carbohydrate and 1 gram of fiber, for a usable carb count of 1 gram; 0 grams protein.

Five-Spice Beef Mop

> 1 1/2 teaspoons Five-Spice Beef Rub (page 49)
>
> 1/2 cup (120 milliliters) oil
>
> 1/2 cup (120 milliliters) water
>
> 1 teaspoon blackstrap molasses

Stir everything together, and use to mop beef you've first seasoned with Five-Spice Beef Rub.

YIELD: This makes 1 cup, or plenty for a slab or two of beef ribs, or a brisket, or what have you.

4 grams of carbohydrate in the whole batch, and there's no way you'll consume anything like the whole batch. I'd call this one free, carb-wise. 0 grams protein.

☀ Five-Spice Barbecue Sauce

The obvious choice if you want a finishing sauce to go with something you've seasoned with the Five-Spice Rub and Mop. Good on anything, though!

3/4 cup (180 grams) Dana's No-Sugar Ketchup (page 30)

1/2 cup (120 milliliters) light beer

1/3 cup (80 milliliters) cider vinegar

1 1/2 tablespoons Splenda

1/4 teaspoon molasses

1 tablespoon Worcestershire sauce

1 clove garlic

1 teaspoon cumin

3/4 teaspoon five-spice powder

Combine everything in a nonreactive saucepan, and let it simmer for 5 minutes or so.

YIELD: Makes roughly 1 3/4 cup, or 14 servings of 2 tablespoons each.

3 grams of carbohydrate, with a trace of fiber, and a trace of protein.

Texas BBQ Brisket Sauce

This is a classic Texas-style barbecue sauce, and it's killer on a slow-smoked hunk of brisket.

　　　2 tablespoons butter

　　　1/2 cup (80 grams) minced onion

　　　1 clove garlic, crushed

　　　1 cup (240 grams) Dana's No-Sugar Ketchup (page 30)

　　　1 tablespoon chili powder

　　　1/4 cup (60 milliliters) Splenda

　　　1/2 teaspoon molasses

　　　2 tablespoons lemon juice

　　　1 tablespoon wine vinegar

　　　2 teaspoons Worcestershire sauce

　　　1 teaspoon liquid smoke flavoring (Colgin makes this;
　　　　　most big grocery stores carry it)

　　　1 teaspoon yellow mustard

　　　1/2 teaspoon salt

　　　1/2 teaspoon pepper

　　　1/4 teaspoon cayenne

Melt the butter in a nonreactive saucepan, and sauté the onion and garlic for 4 or 5 minutes. Add everything else, whisk it smooth, and bring to a simmer over low heat. Let the whole thing simmer for 5 minutes or so.

Hot! Wonderful, too, especially on beef.

YIELD: Makes about 2 cups, or 16 servings of 2 tablespoons each

4 grams of carbohydrate per serving, with 1 gram of fiber, for a usable carb count of 3 grams.

Cajun Rub

- 2 tablespoons celery salt
- 2 tablespoons pepper
- 2 tablespoons Splenda
- 1 1/2 teaspoons garlic powder
- 2 teaspoons dried thyme
- 1 teaspoon ground sage
- 2 teaspoons cayenne
- 1/4 teaspoon blackstrap molasses

This rub needs to be made in a blender, to distribute that sticky molasses throughout the mixture. Put everything but the molasses in your blender. Turn the blender on, and while it's running, drizzle in the 1/4 teaspoon molasses. Turn off the blender, and sprinkle your rub heavily on pork ribs before barbecuing.

YIELD: Makes 5 servings

Each serving will have 5 grams of carbohydrate and 1 gram of fiber, for a usable carb count of 4 grams; 1 gram protein.

Cajun Seasoning

Another recipe borrowed from *500 Low-Carb Recipes*, this keeps well in a shaker with a tight lid (use an old spice shaker) and can be used to give a quick hit of hot-and-spicy flavor to fish, poultry, pork, or—well, just about anything—before grilling.

2 1/2 tablespoons paprika

2 tablespoons salt

2 tablespoons garlic powder

1 tablespoon black pepper

1 tablespoon onion powder

1 tablespoon cayenne pepper

1 tablespoon dried oregano

1 tablespoon dried thyme

Combine all ingredients thoroughly, and store in an airtight container.

YIELD: Makes about 2/3 cup, or 12 servings of 1 tablespoons each

3 grams of carbohydrate and 1 gram fiber, for a usable carb count of 2 grams; 1 gram protein.

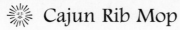 Cajun Rib Mop

½ cup (120 milliliters) cider vinegar

½ cup (120 milliliters) olive oil

1 tablespoon Worcestershire sauce

½ teaspoon cayenne

Simply combine everything, and use to mop pork ribs every 30–45 minutes while barbecuing.

YIELD: Makes just over 1 cup.

10 grams of carbohydrate in the batch, with a trace of fiber and a trace of protein. But you won't actually eat more than 1 tablespoon or so of the mop with a serving, so I'd say no more than 1 gram of carbohydrate per serving.

Cajun Sauce

This is the most complicated sauce in this book to make, but it's marvelous, and makes quite a lot. It's also quite hot—you could mellow it a bit by leaving out the cayenne, I suppose, but it wouldn't really be Cajun, then, would it?

    1 small onion

    1/2 small green bell pepper

    2 celery ribs

    3 cloves garlic

    2 tablespoons olive oil

    1 14-ounce (420-milliliter) can chicken broth

    2/3 cup (160 milliliters) cider vinegar

    3 tablespoons tomato paste

    5 tablespoons spicy mustard

    3 tablespoons Splenda

    1/4 teaspoon blackstrap molasses

    2 tablespoons Dana's No-Sugar Ketchup (page 30)

    1/2 teaspoon chili powder

    1/2 teaspoon cayenne

Chop the onion, pepper, and celery fairly fine—feel free to use your food processor for this; I did! Crush the garlic, too.

In a big saucepan with a heavy bottom, over medium heat, heat the olive oil and add the chopped veggies. Sauté them until everything is soft. Now stir in everything else, turn the burner down, and let the whole thing simmer for a good 15–20 minutes. Spoon over pork—preferably pork you've rubbed with Cajun Seasoning (page 54) and mopped with Cajun Rib Mop (page 55)!

YIELD: Makes about 1 quart, or about 16 servings of 1/4 cup each, though you may eat more!

Each serving will have 4 grams of carbohydrate and 1 gram of fiber, for a usable carb count of 3 grams; 1 gram protein.

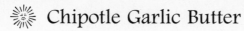 # Chipotle Garlic Butter

Easy, and gives a huge hit of flavor to anything you use it on. Melt it over a steak, use it to baste grilled vegetables or fish—you'll find endless ways to use this!

> 1/4 pound (115 grams) butter at room temperature
>
> 2 chipotle chiles canned in adobo
>
> 1 clove garlic, crushed

Just plunk everything into a food processor with the S-blade in place, and run the processor until everything is well combined.

YIELD: 8 servings of just over 1 tablespoon each

A trace of carbohydrate, a trace of fiber, and a trace of protein.

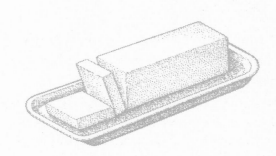

☀ Chipotle Sauce

Essential for Chipotle Cheeseburgers (page 131), but great on a grilled chicken breast, too, or as a dip for lightly cooked, chilled asparagus.

> 3/4 cup (180 grams) mayonnaise
>
> 3 chipotle chiles canned in adobo
>
> 2 tablespoons Dana's No-Sugar Ketchup (page 30)

Measure the mayo into a bowl. Chop up the chipotles quite fine, and stir into the mayonnaise along with the ketchup.

YIELD: 6 servings of 1 generous tablespoon each

1 gram of carbohydrate per serving, with a trace of fiber, 1 gram protein.

✵ Cilantro Chimichurri

This amazingly flavorful herb sauce is wonderful over a grilled steak, especially one that you've seasoned with something a bit hot and spicy.

> 1 bunch cilantro
>
> 5 cloves garlic
>
> 2 tablespoons lime juice
>
> 1/2 small red onion, cut in a few hunks
>
> 1/2 teaspoon red pepper flakes
>
> 2/3 cup (160 milliliters) olive oil

Chop up the cilantro enough to fit it in your food processor, with the S-blade in place. Add everything else but the olive oil, and pulse until everything's fairly finely minced. Scrape the resulting incredibly fragrant mixture into a bowl, and whisk in the olive oil. Spoon over a grilled steak or anything else you can think of!

YIELD: Makes 6 servings of roughly two tablespoons

Each serving will have 3 grams of carbohydrate, with a trace of fiber, and a trace of protein.

Adobo Sauce

This traditional Mexican seasoning is essential for Chicken
Adobo (page 113)!

> 3 cloves garlic
>
> 1 teaspoon salt
>
> 3/4 teaspoon cumin
>
> 1 teaspoon oregano
>
> 1/2 teaspoon pepper
>
> 3/4 cup (180 milliliters) lime juice
>
> 1/4 teaspoon orange extract

Just measure everything, and whisk it together. Use to marinate and baste chicken.

YIELD: Makes just over 3/4 cup, or enough to marinate 1 good-sized cut-up chicken

Assuming 5 servings, each will have 4 grams of carbohydrate, with a trace of
fiber and protein—if you manage to consume all the marinade, which you won't.

☼ Wasabi Baste

Good on any kind of fish or seafood.

2 teaspoons wasabi paste (buy this in tubes in Asian markets or in grocery stores with a good international section)

1 1/2 tablespoons Splenda

1/4 teaspoon blackstrap molasses

2 tablespoons dry sherry

2 tablespoons lime juice

6 tablespoons soy sauce

1/4 teaspoon sesame oil

Just stir everything together, and baste away.

YIELD: A little over 1/2 cup, or enough to baste one darned big salmon, inside and out, as I have reason to know. Figure at least 8 servings.

Each serving will have 2 grams of carbohydrate, a trace of fiber, and 1 gram protein.

Amazing Barbecue Rub

It's the sweetness and the celery undertone that really set this rub apart. One of my favorites on pork or chicken.

1/2 cup (120 milliliters) Splenda

1 teaspoon molasses

3 tablespoons celery salt

2 tablespoons seasoned salt

2 tablespoons onion powder

1 tablespoon garlic powder

1 tablespoon chili powder

1 tablespoon pepper

1/2 teaspoon cayenne

1/4 teaspoon cloves, ground

1 whole bay leaf

YIELD: 18 servings of 1 tablespoon each

3 grams of carbohydrate, with a trace of fiber, and a trace of protein.

☀ Jerk Seasoning

This recipe originally appeared in *500 Low-Carb Recipes*, but it's a classic for grilling, so I thought I'd better include it.

> 1 tablespoon onion flakes
>
> 2 teaspoons ground thyme
>
> 1 teaspoon ground allspice
>
> 1/4 teaspoon ground cinnamon
>
> 1 teaspoon black pepper
>
> 1 teaspoon cayenne pepper
>
> 1 tablespoon onion powder
>
> 2 teaspoons salt
>
> 1/4 teaspoon ground nutmeg
>
> 2 tablespoons Splenda

Combine all the ingredients, and store in an airtight container.

YIELD: Makes 1/3 cup, or 18 servings of 1 teaspoon each

1 gram of carbohydrate, a trace of fiber, and no protein.

Apricosen und Horseradish BBQ Sauce

My German-descended husband named this one. Fruity! Especially good on poultry, but try it on pork as well.

- 1/2 jalapeno
- 1/3 cup (110 grams) low-sugar apricot preserves
- 2 tablespoons bourbon
- 2 tablespoons lime juice
- 1 tablespoon cider vinegar
- 2 tablespoons Dana's No-Sugar Ketchup (page 30)
- 1 1/2 teaspoons soy sauce
- 2 teaspoons Splenda
- 1/4 teaspoon blackstrap molasses
- 1 teaspoon Worcestershire sauce
- 1 tablespoon minced onion
- 2 cloves garlic
- 1/2 teaspoon ginger
- 1 dash salt
- 1 dash pepper
- 2 teaspoons prepared horseradish

Mince the jalapeno (don't forget to wash your hands afterward!). Measure everything into a nonreactive saucepan, and whisk together well. Turn burner to low, and bring to a simmer. Let simmer for 5–10 minutes.

YIELD: 8 servings of 2 tablespoons each

6 grams carbohydrate, with a trace of fiber, and a trace of protein.

☀ Apricot White Wine Sauce

Unlike the Apricosen und Horseradish BBQ Sauce (previous page), this has no tomato note—just apricot, wine, and all those wonderful spices. Like the Apricosen sauce, this is especially good on poultry!

6 tablespoons low-sugar apricot preserves

1/3 cup (80 milliliters) white wine

1/4 medium onion

1/4 teaspoon ginger

1/4 teaspoon cayenne

1/8 teaspoon allspice

1/4 cup (16 grams) tarragon

1/4 teaspoon turmeric

1/8 teaspoon cardamom

3 tablespoons Dijon or spicy brown mustard

Measure everything into a nonreactive saucepan, and whisk together well. Simmer on low for 5–10 minutes.

YIELD: Roughly 1 1/4 cups, or 10 servings of 2 tablespoons each

5 grams carbohydrate, with a trace of fiber, and 1 gram of protein.

☀ Beer~Molasses Marinade

Great for ribs, or any pork!

> 1 1/2 (360 milliliters) cups water
>
> 12-ounce (360-milliliter) can light beer
>
> 1 teaspoon blackstrap molasses
>
> 1/4 cup (60 milliliters) Splenda
>
> 1 tablespoon dried thyme
>
> 1 tablespoon salt
>
> 1 whole bay leaf
>
> 1/2 teaspoon pepper

Combine everything in a nonreactive bowl or pan. Marinate your meat in a big zip-lock bag, or shallow pan, large enough to hold the meat. Either way, let it marinade for several hours before cooking.

YIELD: Makes about 3 cups—double it if you need to

18 grams of carbohydrate in the whole batch, with 2 grams of fiber, for a usable carb count of 16 grams; 1 gram protein. But remember, this is a marinade, so you won't consume anything like the whole batch. I'd count only 1 or 2 grams of carb per serving.

☀ Bourbon-Molasses Barbecue Sauce

Bourbon-based sauces are particularly popular on pork ribs, but they're also good on chicken.

>   1/4 cup (40 grams) minced onion
>
>   1 tablespoon oil
>
>   1/2 cup (120 milliliters) red wine vinegar
>
>   1 teaspoon blackstrap molasses
>
>   1 cup (240 grams) Dana's No-Sugar Ketchup (page 30)
>
>   1/4 cup (60 milliliters) plus 1 tablespoon Splenda
>
>   2 tablespoons water
>
>   1/4 cup (60 milliliters) bourbon

In a nonreactive saucepan, sauté the onion in the oil for 4 or 5 minutes. Stir in everything else, and let it all simmer for 5 minutes or so.

YIELD: Makes about 2 cups, or 16 servings of 2 tablespoons each

5 grams carbohydrate, 1 gram fiber, for a usable carb count of 4 grams; a trace of protein.

Bourbon Maple Mop

1/4 cup (60 milliliters) oil

1/4 cup (60 milliliters) water

2 tablespoons bourbon

1 tablespoon sugar-free pancake syrup

1 teaspoon barbecue spice or Classic Barbecue Rub (page 31)

Simply combine all ingredients in a nonreactive bowl or saucepan, and stir.

YIELD: Enough for a slab or two of ribs.

Not counting the polyols in the sugar-free pancake syrup, there's only a trace of carbohydrate in the whole batch. No fiber, no protein.

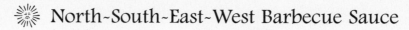 North~South~East~West Barbecue Sauce

This is perhaps the most unusual barbecue sauce in this book, and one of the best. The flavor is evenly balanced between maple, orange, bourbon, and cayenne, giving it flavors from virtually every region of the country. Wonderful on pork or chicken.

2 tablespoons butter

2 tablespoons minced onion

1/2 cup (120 milliliters) bourbon

1/2 cup (120 grams) Dana's No-Sugar Ketchup (page 30)

1/4 cup (60 milliliters) cider vinegar

1/4 teaspoon orange extract

1/4 cup (60 milliliters) sugar-free pancake syrup

1 tablespoon blackstrap molasses

2 tablespoons Splenda

1 tablespoon Worcestershire sauce

1/4 green pepper, minced

1/4 teaspoon cayenne

In a nonreactive saucepan, over low heat, melt the butter and sauté the onion for 5 minutes or so. Add everything else, stir it up, and bring it to a simmer. Let it cook for 7–10 minutes.

YIELD: Makes roughly 1 cup, or 8 servings of 2 tablespoons each

8 grams of carb, with 1 gram of fiber, for a usable carb count of 7 grams. This count does not include the polyols in the sugar-free pancake syrup.

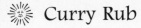 Curry Rub

I invented this for poultry, but it would be good on lamb, too!

> 1 tablespoon curry powder
>
> 1 1/2 teaspoons onion salt
>
> 1 1/2 teaspoons garlic salt
>
> 1 teaspoon celery salt

Just combine everything, and sprinkle it on chicken, lamb, or what have you.

This is just about enough for 1 chicken of about 3 1/2–4 pounds (2 kilograms), so feel free to double, triple, or quadruple this recipe, if you like.

YIELD: This whole batch—2 tablespoons plus 1 teaspoon worth—contains 6 grams of carbohydrate, of which 4 grams are fiber, for 2 grams of usable carb. So, if you figure that 1 chicken will serve 5 people, each will get less than 1/2 gram carbohydrate. 1 gram protein in the whole batch.

Peppery Lamb Rub

2 tablespoons pepper

1 tablespoon Splenda

1 tablespoon salt or Vege-Sal

1 tablespoon garlic powder

1/4 teaspoon allspice

1/4 teaspoon molasses

Put everything but the molasses in your blender. Turn on the blender, drizzle in the molasses, and let everything blend for 30 seconds. Stop the blender and stir the mixture down from the sides if needed.

YIELD: Makes about 5 tablespoons of rub

Each will have 3 grams of carbohydrate and 1 gram of fiber, for a usable carb count of 2 grams; 1 gram protein.

Lamb Mop

1/2 cup (120 milliliters) beer, light

1/4 cup (60 milliliters) oil

3 tablespoons vinegar

2 tablespoons Worcestershire sauce

1 tablespoon Peppery Lamb Rub (page 71)

Just measure everything into a nonreactive bowl or saucepan, and stir it up.

YIELD: Makes about 1 cup.

13 grams of carb and 1 gram of fiber for the whole batch, but you won't end up consuming anything like all of this. I'd doubt very much whether you'll end up with more than 2 grams per serving from this mop.

Dixie Belle Rub

This Southern-style rub is particularly good on pork or chicken.

2 tablespoons pepper

2 tablespoons paprika

2 tablespoons Splenda

2 teaspoons salt

1 tablespoon dry mustard

1 teaspoon cayenne

2 teaspoons garlic powder

Just stir everything together, and rub on ribs, a pork shoulder, chicken, or what have you!

YIELD: Make 1/2 cup, or 8 tablespoons

Each serving will have 3 grams of carbohydrate and 1 gram of fiber, for a usable carb count of 2 grams; 1 gram protein.

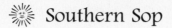 Southern Sop

The perfect southern mopping sauce to use with your Dixie Belle Rub.

> 1/2 cup (120 milliliters) cider vinegar
>
> 1/2 tablespoon pepper
>
> 1 teaspoon salt
>
> 1 teaspoon Worcestershire sauce
>
> 1 teaspoon paprika
>
> 1 tablespoon Dixie Belle Rub (page 72)
>
> 1/4 cup (60 milliliters) water
>
> 1/4 cup (60 milliliters) oil

Just combine everything, and use to baste meat or chicken during smoking.

YIELD: Makes a little over 1 cup, or plenty for your ribs or shoulder or whatever you're barbecuing

14 grams of carbohydrate in the whole batch, with 2 grams of fiber, for a usable carb count of 12 grams; 1 gram of protein. However, you won't use all of this sauce, even for a couple of slabs of ribs, and a couple of slabs will serve 15–20 people. Figure that each diner will get no more than 1–2 grams of usable carb from this mop.

☀ Sweet and Spicy Mustard Sauce

If you like honey-mustard dressing, give this barbecue sauce a try.

> 1/2 cup (125 grams) spicy brown mustard
>
> 1/4 cup (60 milliliters) Splenda
>
> 1/2 teaspoon molasses
>
> 1/8 teaspoon instant coffee crystals
>
> 1 teaspoon Worcestershire sauce
>
> 1 teaspoon hot sauce
>
> 2 tablespoons water

Just whisk everything together in a nonreactive saucepan over low heat. Bring it to a simmer, and let it cook just a few minutes to blend the flavors.

YIELD: Makes just under 1 cup, or about 7 servings of 2 tablespoons each

3 grams of carb per serving, with a trace of fiber, and 1 gram of protein.

☀ Sweet Spice Islands Rub

Allspice, ginger, and cloves set this rub apart from the pack. I like this on pork, but it would be great on chicken or duck—lamb, too. You'll need to have Classic Barbecue Rub on hand, of course.

> 1/4 cup (60 milliliters) Splenda
>
> 2 tablespoons Classic Barbecue Rub (page 31)
>
> 1 tablespoon seasoned salt
>
> 1/4 teaspoon allspice
>
> 1/8 teaspoon ginger
>
> 1/8 teaspoon clove, ground
>
> 1/4 teaspoon cayenne
>
> 1/2 teaspoon black pepper

Just stir everything together, and rub on whatever you feel like barbecuing!

YIELD: Makes about 7 servings of 1 tablespoon each

2 grams of carbohydrate, a trace of fiber, and a trace of protein.

☀ Sweet Spice Islands Sauce

For use with the Sweet Spice Islands Rub, of course!

   2 tablespoons butter

   1/4 cup (40 grams) minced onion

   1 clove garlic, crushed

   1/3 cup (80 grams) Dana's No-Sugar Ketchup (page 30)

   1 tablespoon cider vinegar

   1 tablespoon lemon juice

   1 tablespoon Worcestershire sauce

   1 tablespoon sugar-free imitation honey

   1 tablespoon Splenda

   1 tablespoon Sweet Spice Islands Rub (page 74)

Melt the butter over lowest heat in a nonreactive saucepan, and sauté the onion and garlic in it for 4 or 5 minutes. Whisk in everything else, bring to a simmer, and let it cook for 5 minutes or so.

YIELD: Makes a little over 1 cup, or about 9 servings of 2 tablespoons each

9 grams of carbohydrate per serving, but 2 grams of that are the polyols in the imitation honey, and 1 gram is fiber, so count 6 grams of usable carb; 1 gram protein.

☀ Florida Sunshine Tangerine Barbecue Sauce

The name of this sauce is partly from the tangerine note, which is unusual and delicious, but also from the fact that this sauce is at least as hot as the Florida sun! Especially good on poultry.

1 12-ounce (360-milliliter) can Diet-Rite tangerine soda

1/4 cup (60 milliliters) Splenda

1 tablespoon chili powder

2 teaspoons black pepper

1 teaspoon ginger

1 teaspoon dry mustard

1 teaspoon onion salt

4 cloves garlic, crushed

1/2 teaspoon cayenne

1/2 teaspoon coriander

1/2 teaspoon red pepper flakes

1 whole bay leaf

1/2 cup (120 milliliters) cider vinegar

1 tablespoon sugar-free imitation honey

1 tablespoon Worcestershire sauce

3/4 cup (180 grams) Dana's No-Sugar Ketchup (page 30)

Pour the soda into a nonreactive saucepan, and turn the heat under it to medium-low. While that's heating, measure the other ingredients into the sauce. By the time you get to the ketchup, it should be simmering. Whisk everything together until smooth, and let it simmer over lowest heat for a good 10–15 minutes.

YIELD: Makes about 3 cups, or 24 servings of 2 tablespoons each

Only 3 grams of carb per serving, with a trace of fiber, a trace of polyols, a trace of protein.

 Spicy Citrus Butter

This is good melted over grilled fish or seafood, chicken, vegetables, even a steak. Actually, it's hard to think of what it's not good on!

> 6 tablespoons butter
>
> 2 jalapenos
>
> 2 tablespoons Splenda
>
> 2 tablespoons lemon juice
>
> 1/2 teaspoon orange extract

Have your butter at room temperature. Put it in the food processor, with the S-blade in place. Seed your jalapenos, and whack each one into several pieces; dump them into the food processor, then wash your hands! Add everything else; then run the food processor until the jalapenos are finely minced. Scoop a dollop over your food, hot off the grill.

If you'd like to use this as a baste, you can do it this way, instead: Put the butter in a saucepan, over the lowest possible heat. Seed the jalapenos, and mince them as fine as you can. Add them to the butter, and wash your hands. As the butter liquefies, whisk in the Splenda, lemon juice, and orange extract. Keep it warm on a corner of your grill (not over direct heat), and use it to baste fish fillets, seafood, or chicken breasts.

YIELD: Makes 8 servings of a little over 1 tablespoon each

1 gram of carbohydrate, a trace of fiber, and a trace of protein.

☀ Hoisin Sauce

This is another repeat from *500 Low-Carb Recipes*, only doubled. Hoisin is a traditional Chinese barbecue sauce. It's usually made from fermented soybean paste, but that has lots of sugar in it—this peanut butter–based version is surprisingly good.

> 1/2 cup (120 milliliters) soy sauce
>
> 1/4 cup (60 grams) creamy natural peanut butter
>
> 1/4 cup (60 milliliters) Splenda
>
> 4 teaspoons white vinegar
>
> 2 cloves garlic, crushed
>
> 4 teaspoons toasted sesame oil
>
> 1/4 teaspoon Chinese five-spice powder

Put everything in your blender, and run it until everything is smooth and well combined. Store in a snap-top container.

YIELD: Makes roughly 2/3 cup, or 6 servings of 2 tablespoons each

5 grams of carb, 1 gram of fiber, for a usable carb count of 4 grams; 4 grams protein.

chapter three

Pork

Pork is the first of the meats in this book for a very good reason: In most of the country, the words "barbecue" and "pork" are virtually synonymous. Spare ribs, pork chops, shoulders, even pig roasts (going, as we say, the whole hog)— barbecue fanatics everywhere rely on pork for tender, succulent, unbelievably fragrant and tasty eating.

For some reason which escapes me, pork has a bad reputation, nutritionally speaking. It's a bum rap. Pork is extremely nutritious and is a particularly good source of both niacin and potassium. It's also a good source of monounsaturated fats—that's right, the same heart-healthy fats you find in olive oil! So let's split a slab, shall we?

☀ Absolutely Classic Barbecued Ribs

This is what most of us think of when we think "barbecued ribs," and a beautiful thing it is, too.

> 1 slab pork spare ribs, about 7 pounds (3 kilograms)
>
> 1/2 cup (60 grams) Classic Barbecue Rub (page 31), divided
>
> 1/2 cup (120 milliliters) oil
>
> 1/2 cup (120 milliliters) water
>
> 1 cup (240 grams) Kansas City Barbecue Sauce (page 32)

First, fire up that grill! Set it up for indirect smoking, as described in chapter 1.

Sprinkle your ribs heavily on either side with the Classic Barbecue Rub. Then, when your grill is hot and your charcoal, if any, is well covered with ash, throw your ribs on the grill on the side away from the fire. Smoke 'em for a good 6 hours at 225°F (110°C), following the instructions in chapter 1.

Okay, your ribs are in the hot smoke. Put the oil and water in a small pan or bowl, and stir in 2 tablespoons of the Classic Barbecue Rub. After your ribs have smoked for about 30–45 minutes, use this simple mop to baste them every time you add fresh chips or chunks to the fire. Turn the ribs over every 60–90 minutes.

Come the last 20 minutes of your cooking time, baste your ribs well with the Kansas City Barbecue Sauce, and put them directly over the fire for 10 minutes per side, to crisp them a little. Serve with cold light beer, slaw, extra sauce, and a big roll of paper towels!

Feel free to use this same basic method with any rub and any sauce!

YIELD: About 8–9 servings

Assuming 8, each will have 10 grams of carbohydrate with 2 grams of fiber, for a usable carb count of 8 grams; 49 grams of protein.

Bauer Family Ribs

My cyberpal Jerry Randall Bauer came through town with his wife and son, so they came by for a cookout, and a fine time was had by all. Here's how I fixed ribs that day:

☀ Bauer Family Rib Boil

To purists, the notion of simmering ribs briefly to cut the smoking time is cheating—absolutely anathema. Me, I find that simmering ribs not only cuts the cooking time in half, but it makes them moister in the bargain, so the heck with the purists!

> 6 quarts (5.7 liters) water
>
> 2 tablespoons salt
>
> 2 teaspoons poultry seasoning
>
> 1/2 teaspoon orange extract
>
> 1 tablespoon Splenda
>
> 1 slab pork spareribs, about 6 pounds (3 kilograms)

Combine everything in a large kettle. Cut your slab in half, if you need to, to fit it into the kettle. Bring it to a simmer, and let the whole thing simmer for 20 minutes; then proceed with the barbecuing.

YIELD: At least six servings, depending on meatiness of your ribs.

In the entire batch, there are 3 grams of carbohydrate, but since you will pour the vast majority of liquid down the drain, I'd call this carb-free.

Bauer Family Rib Mop

Scoop out 1/2 cup of the Bauer Family Rib Boil, and combine with 1/2 cup oil. Use to baste ribs during slow smoking, as described in chapter 1. Smoke the simmered ribs over an indirect fire for at least 3 hours, or until very tender.

Bauer Family Rib Sauce

This sauce is unusual in that it has no tomato base at all. The main note is apricot, with a bit of heat and the unexpected zing of mint. Combine it with the orange/herb note of the rib boil and mop, and you've got a good, round, fruity taste that really complements the pork.

> 2 tablespoons butter
>
> 1/4 cup (40 grams) minced onion
>
> 1 clove garlic
>
> 2 teaspoons chili garlic paste
>
> 1/4 cup (60 milliliters) white wine vinegar
>
> 1/4 cup (80 grams) low-sugar apricot preserves
>
> 1 tablespoon Splenda
>
> 2 tablespoons chopped fresh mint

Melt the butter in a medium-sized saucepan, and sauté the minced onion in it until soft. Add everything else but the mint, and simmer for 5 minutes. Turn off the heat, and stir in the chopped mint. Use to baste your Bauer Family Ribs during the last 20 minutes of cooking, and serve any leftover sauce with the ribs.

YIELD: Enough for 1 slab, or about 5 servings

Assuming 5 servings, each will have 7 grams of carbohydrate, with a trace of fiber, and a trace of protein.

☀ Simple Marinated Ribs

Why is this recipe for a half-slab of ribs? Because there are only two of us in my household, that's why! Feel free to double the marinade and use a whole slab if you like—but you'll want to cut the slab into two pieces, so it'll fit into a zipper-lock bag. What with the marinade/mop, these have plenty of flavor without a finishing sauce, but feel free to use one if you really want to.

> 1/2 cup olive oil
>
> 1/2 cup (120 milliliters) cider vinegar
>
> 1 tablespoon Splenda
>
> 1 tablespoon spicy mustard
>
> 1/2 teaspoon grated gingerroot
>
> 3 pounds (1.5 kilograms) pork spareribs—about half a slab

Combine everything but the ribs and the oil. Put the ribs in a large zipper-lock plastic bag, pour the vinegar mixture over it, and seal the bag, pressing out the air as you go. Turn the bag a couple of times to make sure the whole surface of the meat comes in contact with the marinade. Throw your ribs in the fridge, and let 'em marinate all day, or even overnight, turning now and then when you open the fridge anyway and think of it.

Six hours before dinner, get your fire going for indirect smoking, as described in chapter 1. When the fire is ready, pour off the marinade into a bowl, and add 1/2 cup of oil—this is your mopping sauce. Throw your ribs on the grill, and smoke them for 5–6 hours or until quite tender, basting every 30–45 minutes (or when you add more chips or chunks to the fire) with the mop you made from the marinade.

YIELD: 4 servings

Each serving will have 2 grams of carbohydrate and a trace of fiber if you finish the marinade, which you won't—I'd count 1 gram, myself; 36 grams of protein.

☀ Apple-Maple Brined Ribs

Okay, I admit it. This is not a spontaneous recipe; it takes forever! Quite simple, though, and these ribs taste wonderful with no other seasoning at all. This recipe is for a half-slab, so feel free to double it.

> 1/2 cup (100 grams) salt
>
> 7 cups (1.7 liters) hot water
>
> 2 cups (480 milliliters) cider vinegar
>
> 1/2 cup (120 milliliters) Splenda
>
> 1/2 cup (120 milliliters) sugar-free pancake syrup
>
> 1 1/2 teaspoons cracked black pepper
>
> 1/2 slab pork spare ribs, about 4 pounds (2 kilograms)

Dissolve the salt in the hot water, then stir in everything else but the ribs. Put your ribs in something shallow, flat, and made of a nonreactive material—you may want to cut your slab into a few pieces to fit it in. Pour the brine over the ribs, making sure they're submerged by at least a little bit. Stash them in the fridge, and let them sit for 3–4 hours.

Six hours before you want to eat your brined ribs, start your grill for indirect cooking—build a charcoal fire to one side, or light only one burner of your gas grill. Pull your ribs out of the brine and pat them dry. Reserve 1/2 cup of the brine; discard the rest. Rub the surface of the ribs with a little oil.

When your fire is ready, put the ribs over the side of the grill not over the fire, and add soaked wood chips to the fire—apple wood would be especially appropriate, but I've used other chips and gotten good results. Smoke the ribs according to the directions in chapter 1, for a good 6 hours, adding wood chips whenever the smoke dies down.

What do you do with that 1/2 cup reserved brine? Mix it with 1/2 cup oil, and use it to baste the ribs while they're smoking, every time you add more chips or chunks.

You can add other seasonings or a sauce to these if you like, but I like them with just salt and pepper. The brine/mop adds a lovely flavor of its own and makes these ribs wonderfully juicy!

YIELD: 5–6 servings

If you drank the brine, you'd get a substantial quantity of carbohydrate (7 or 8 grams) but you discard most of the brine, of course. Count 1 to 2 grams per serving, at most; 32 grams of protein.

 Orange Brined Ribs

16 ounces (480 milliliters) orange-flavored $Fruit_2O$

1 tablespoon salt

2 cloves garlic

1/8 teaspoon blackstrap molasses

1 1/2 teaspoons soy sauce

3 pounds (1.5 kilograms) country-style pork ribs

1/2 cup (120 milliliters) olive oil

Dissolve the salt in the $Fruit_2O$—heating the $Fruit_2O$ a bit will help the salt dissolve. Stir in everything else but the ribs and oil. Set aside 1 tablespoon of the brine to use in the Orange Rib Glaze (page 86). Put your ribs in a shallow nonreactive dish, and pour the brine over them, making sure the ribs are submerged by at least a little bit. Put the whole thing in the fridge, and let the ribs soak in the brine for 4–5 hours.

Five to 6 hours before you want to eat, prepare the grill for indirect cooking—build a charcoal fire to one side, or light only one burner of your gas grill. When the fire is ready, pull the ribs out, pour off 1/2 cup of the brine into one container, and pour 1 tablespoon of brine into another if you plan to make the Orange Rib Glaze, which follows. Discard the rest of the brine. Pat the ribs dry, and rub them with a little oil. Put them on the grill, and add soaked wood chips to the fire. Cover the grill, and smoke the ribs for 5–6 hours according to the directions in chapter 1.

Combine the 1/2 cup of reserved brine with 1/2 cup of oil, and use to mop your ribs every time you add chips or chunks to the fire.

I like to coat these with Orange Rib Glaze in the last 20 minutes before they come off the grill, but serve them with whatever sauce or seasoning you like!

YIELD: 5 servings

Exclusive of any sauce you might add, these are virtually carb-free! 32 grams of protein.

Orange Rib Glaze

    1 tablespoon sugar-free imitation honey

    1 tablespoon orange brine

    1/4 teaspoon orange extract

    1/2 teaspoon soy sauce

    1 clove garlic, crushed

    1/2 teaspoon grated gingerroot

Simply stir everything together, and brush evenly over Orange Brined Ribs (page 85) in the last 20 minutes of cooking. This is just enough to make a thin glaze over the ribs, not enough to spoon over them at the table—but trust me, if you've used the brine and the mop, you'll have plenty of flavor.

YIELD: 5 servings

Each serving has 3 grams of carbohydrate, exclusive of the polyols in the imitation honey; a trace of fiber; a trace of protein.

 # Cajun Barbecued Pork

Hot! Not for the timid, but complex and delicious.

    4 pounds (2 kilograms) country-style pork ribs

    1 batch Cajun Rub (page 53)

    1 batch Cajun Rib Mop (page 55)

    2/3 cup (160 grams) Cajun Sauce (page 56)

Set up your grill for indirect smoking, as described in chapter 1. Rub your country-style ribs all over with the Cajun Rub, and place them on the grill. Smoke them for 30–45 minutes, then start to baste them with the Cajun Rib Mop every time you open the grill to add more chips or chunks. Smoke for 3– 4 hours, at least, or until an instant-read thermometer registers 170°F (80°C). Serve with the Cajun Sauce.

YIELD: 6 servings

Each serving will have 7 grams of carbohydrate and 1 gram of fiber, for a usable carb count of 6 grams; 36 grams protein.

☀ Carolina Pulled Pork

In much of the country, spareribs are the favorite part of the pig to barbecue. But in the Carolinas, barbecue means pork shoulder (or sometimes even the whole hog!), smoked for ages until it's tender and juicy. Then the meat is cut or pulled off the bone and combined with one of a few different kinds of sauces, depending on the region. The whole process takes a lot of time (though not a tremendous amount of work), but the results are nothing short of spectacular!

> 1 pork picnic shoulder, about 4 pounds (2 kilograms)
>
> Oil
>
> Salt and pepper
>
> Barbecue rub of choice (optional)

This is way too simple. Get your fire going first, with your grill set up for indirect smoking as described in chapter 1. Then rub the pork shoulder all over with a little oil, salt and pepper it, and sprinkle it liberally with barbecue rub if desired. It's a good idea to insert a meat thermometer into the center of the thickest part of the meat, taking care not to let it touch the bone.

Then put that hunk of pork on your grill, fatty side up, and smoke it for a long, long time—6–7 hours. (Don't try simmering this like you might a rack of ribs you wanted to speed up. If you don't have the time, make something else.) Make sure you replace your chips or chunks when necessary, so you get plenty of good smoky flavor, and take care to keep the temperature between 200°F and 225°F (95°C and 110°C). (Lower isn't disastrous, but it can stretch out your cooking time even further. Higher, and your meat will grill, not smoke.) When the internal temperature is between 170°F and 180°F (80°C and 85°C), your pork is done. Take it off the grill, and let it rest for 10 minutes before cutting it up.

Okay, 10 minutes are up! Cut or pull the pork off the bone; you can discard the bone. Pull or cut off the outside fat. Then, either chop up the meat or pull it apart with two forks until it's in shreds. Now mix it with about 2/3 cup (160 grams) Piedmont Mustard Sauce (page 40), Eastern Carolina Vinegar Sauce (page 41), or Lexington-Style Barbecue Sauce (page 42).

How to serve your pulled pork? After all, it's usually served on a bun, and we're sure not going to eat it that way. Well, you can just eat it with a fork by itself, of course, and it will be extremely nice. However, since Carolina barbecue sandwiches are usually topped with coleslaw, why not serve yourself a big pile of coleslaw, top it with pulled pork, and eat the two together as a main-dish salad?

YIELD: A 4-pound (2-kilogram) shoulder will yield about 6 servings

The carb count will depend on which sauce you choose; the meat itself is pretty much carb-free; 39 grams of protein.

☀ Bourbon Mustard Pork Ribs

No rub or finishing sauce needed—the marinade/baste alone makes these mustardy-tangy-sweet.

> 1 cup (225 milliliters) bourbon
>
> 1 cup (225 milliliters) oil
>
> 1 tablespoon molasses
>
> 1 cup (250 grams) spicy brown mustard
>
> 2 tablespoons dried sage
>
> 2 teaspoons salt or Vege-Sal
>
> 2 teaspoons pepper
>
> 1 tablespoon dried thyme
>
> 1 cup (225 milliliters) Splenda
>
> 1 slab pork spare ribs, about 6–7 pounds (3 kilograms)

Combine everything but the ribs. Cut the ribs in two, so they'll fit in a pot—use a nonreactive one, only big enough to fit the ribs. Pour the bourbon mixture over them, and let them marinate for several hours, at least.

Now you get to make a choice: to simmer, or not to simmer? I like to simmer—put the pot over a burner set on medium-low, bring the marinade to a simmer, and let the ribs cook for 25–30 minutes.

Either way, set up your grill for indirect smoking, as described in chapter 1. If you've simmered your ribs, smoke them for 3 hours. If you haven't, smoke them for 5–6 hours. Either way, baste them with the bourbon-mustard marinade every 30–45 minutes while they're smoking, basting them for the last time at least 15–20 minutes before pulling the ribs out of the hot smoke.

These don't need any sauce at all, not even the boiled-down marinade—just eat 'em as is.

YIELD: 8 servings

If you consumed all the marinade/baste, you'd get 8 grams of carb per serving, with 1 gram of fiber, but you won't consume all of the marinade/baste! Estimating generously that you'll eat two-thirds of the bourbon-mustard mixture, you'll get 6 grams of carb per serving, with a trace of fiber, and the count may actually be lower than that; 39 grams of protein.

☀ Chinese Pork

Pork is the most popular meat in China, and this is a de-carbed version of a classic Chinese seasoning. Feel free to do this with spareribs instead.

1/2 cup (120 milliliters) soy sauce

1/4 cup (60 milliliters) sherry

1 clove garlic

2 tablespoons Splenda

1 tablespoon grated gingerroot

3 pounds (1.5 kilograms) country-style pork ribs

1/4 cup (60 milliliters) oil

Mix together everything from the soy sauce through the gingerroot. Put the ribs in a shallow, nonreactive pan or a zipper-lock bag, and pour the marinade over them. If you're using a bag, press out the air and seal it. Either way, turn the ribs to coat. Stick your ribs in the fridge and let them marinate for at least a few hours.

Okay, marinating time's up. Pour off the marinade and reserve. Put your ribs in a heavy-bottomed saucepan, just barely cover with water, and add half the marinade. Bring to a simmer, and simmer your ribs for 45 minutes. When they're getting on toward the end of simmering time, start your grill. Mix the oil with the leftover marinade.

Put your ribs over a medium-low charcoal fire or gas grill, and grill slowly over direct heat, basting often with the marinade-oil mixture, until quite tender—about another 45 minutes.

YIELD: 6 servings

If you consumed all of the marinade, each serving would have 4 grams of carbohydrate, and a trace of fiber. Since you don't, figure closer to 3 grams per serving; 28 grams of protein.

☀ Hoisin Basted Ribs

Another Chinese-influenced version of ribs. You'll have to make the low-carb Hoisin Sauce first, but then, it's a nice thing to have on hand anyway.

> 1 slab pork spareribs, about 6 pounds (3 kilograms)
>
> 3/4 cup (180 grams) Hoisin Sauce (page 78)
>
> 1/4 cup (60 milliliters) dry sherry
>
> 3 tablespoons sugar-free imitation honey
>
> 4 cloves garlic, crushed
>
> 1 teaspoon grated gingerroot
>
> 1 1/2 tablespoons Splenda
>
> Oil
>
> Salt and pepper

Simmer your ribs first for this one—put them in a kettle big enough to hold them, and cover them with water. (You can add a little soy sauce and Splenda, if you like.) Bring them to a simmer, and let them simmer for 30–45 minutes.

While that's happening, get your fire going, especially if you're using charcoal. You'll want your fire medium-low.

Next, put together your sauce, simply by putting the low-carb Hoisin Sauce, sherry, imitation honey, garlic, and gingerroot in the blender, and running it till everything is well combined.

Okay, your ribs are done simmering. Pull them out, pat them dry with paper towels, and give them a nice massage with a little oil. Salt and pepper them, and put them over the fire—we're directly grilling them this time, instead of slow smoking them. Put them meaty-side down, close the grill, and let them cook for 20 minutes. Flip them over, re-close the grill, and let them go another 40–45 minutes.

About 20 minutes before cooking time is up, baste your ribs with the Hoisin Sauce, and baste 'em again 10 minutes later. Serve the rest of the sauce at the table.

YIELD: 9 servings

Each serving will have 5 grams carbohydrate and a trace of fiber, not including the polyols in the imitation honey; 35 grams protein.

☀ Lemon-Garlic-Jalapeno Pork Steaks

    1 whole jalapeno, minced

    1/4 cup (60 milliliters) olive oil

    2 tablespoons lemon juice

    2 cloves garlic, crushed

    1/4 teaspoon cumin

    1 teaspoon adobo seasoning (look for this in the spice aisle)

    1 1/2 pounds (700 grams) pork shoulder steaks

Simply stir together everything but the pork. Put the pork on a plate with a rim—a glass pie plate is ideal—and pour the sauce over it. Turn the steaks over once or twice to coat, and let the steaks sit for at least 30 minutes before grilling.

Grill over a medium charcoal or gas fire, holding down flare-ups with your squirt bottle, for 8–10 minutes per side. Baste once or twice during cooking with the marinade from the pie plate.

YIELD: 3 servings

Each serving will have 2 grams carbohydrate, a trace of fiber, and 30 grams of protein.

 # Peach-Orange Brined Pork Chops with Herb Rub

1 16-ounce (480-milliliter) bottle peach-flavored Fruit$_2$O

1 tablespoon salt

1/4 teaspoon blackstrap molasses

1/4 teaspoon orange extract

4 pork chops, totaling about 1 1/2 pounds (700 grams)

1 clove garlic

1 tablespoon olive oil

1 teaspoon ground rosemary

1/2 teaspoon ground or rubbed sage

1/2 teaspoon dried marjoram

1/8 teaspoon cayenne

In a flat, shallow dish—a good-sized glass casserole is perfect—combine the Fruit$_2$O, salt, molasses, and orange extract. Stir until the salt is dissolved. (Heating helps with this—you can open the bottle of Fruit$_2$O and microwave it for a minute before pouring it in the dish, or you can microwave the whole batch of brine, if your dish is microwavable. Neither is essential, it just helps the salt dissolve.) Place the chops in the brine (make sure it's cooled to lukewarm, first), make sure they're submerged, and stick the whole thing in the fridge. Let 'em sit for about 3 hours.

Okay, time to grill your pork. First start your grill heating—set a gas grill to medium-high; with a charcoal grill you'll want to let your coals cook down to a medium heat. Crush the garlic and mix it with the olive oil in a small dish. In another dish combine all your herbs. Then pull the chops out of the brine and put them on a plate; discard the brine. Pat your chops dry. Rub them all over with the garlic and olive oil mixture, then with the herb mixture.

Grill chops about 12 minutes per side, or until there's no pink left in the center, then serve.

YIELD: 4 servings

Each serving will have 1 gram of carbohydrate, a trace of fiber, 26 grams of protein.

☀ Cajun Pork Chops
with Grilled Pineapple Mint Chutney

> 2 pounds (1 kilogram) pork chops, about 1" (2.5 centimeters) thick
>
> 1/4 cup (30 grams) Cajun Seasoning, either homemade (page 54)
>   or purchased
>
> Grilled Pineapple Mint Chutney (recipe follows)

Simply sprinkle both sides of your chops liberally with the Cajun Seasoning, and grill over a medium flame until done. Top with Grilled Pineapple Mint Chutney, and serve.

YIELD: 6 servings

Without the Pineapple Mint Chutney, each serving has 4 grams of carb and 1 gram of fiber, for a usable carb count of 3 grams; 24 grams protein.

☀ Grilled Pineapple Mint Chutney

Don't expect there to be piles and piles of chutney on each serving; I've kept the quantity small to keep the carb count low. This is just enough to be a nice foil to the spicy-hot chops. The grilling intensifies the flavor of the pineapple.

- 1 cup (160 grams) fresh pineapple chunks
- 3 tablespoons Splenda
- 2 tablespoons white vinegar
- 2 tablespoons lemon juice
- 1 tablespoon low-sugar apricot preserves
- 4 tablespoons chopped fresh mint

You'll need skewers—if you use bamboo ones, soak them in water for at least 30 minutes ahead of time. Thread the pineapple onto the skewers, and grill over a medium fire until softened and browned a bit. Remove from fire.

Push the pineapple off the skewers into a nonreactive saucepan, and add the Splenda, vinegar, lemon juice, and low-sugar apricot preserves. Put over low heat, and let the whole thing simmer for 5 minutes or so. When the pineapple is soft enough, mash it a bit with a fork or potato masher. Chop up your mint, stir it in at the last minute, and spoon the chutney over your pork chops.

YIELD: 6 servings

Each serving will have 6 grams of carb and 1 gram of fiber, for a usable carb count of 5 grams; a trace of protein.

☀ Apple-Mustard Pork Steaks

I've always loved apples and pork together, and the mustard just makes the whole thing better!

        1 pound (500 grams) pork shoulder steaks

        1/4 cup (60 milliliters) cider vinegar

        2 tablespoons Splenda

        1 clove garlic

        2 teaspoons soy sauce

        1/2 teaspoon grated gingerroot

        2 teaspoons spicy brown mustard

Place your pork steaks on a plate with a rim. Mix together everything else, and pour it over the steaks. Turn the steaks once or twice to coat, then let them sit for 30 minutes or so. Meanwhile, get your grill going.

Okay, fire's ready! Grill over a medium gas grill or well-ashed coals for about 8–10 minutes per side, basting several times with the marinade. If you like, you can boil any leftover marinade and pour it over the steaks before serving.

YIELD: 2 servings

Each serving will have 5 grams of carbohydrate, a trace of fiber, 30 grams of protein.

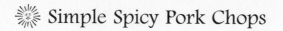 # Simple Spicy Pork Chops

3 tablespoons olive oil

1 clove garlic

1 ½ pounds (700 grams) pork chops, about 1" (2.5 centimeters) thick

1 tablespoon chili powder

1 teaspoon ground coriander

Measure out the olive oil; crush the garlic and stir it into the oil. Rub the chops thoroughly with the garlicky olive oil. Stir the chili powder and coriander together, and sprinkle over both sides of the chops. Grill over well-ashed coals, or on a gas grill set to medium-low, about 10 minutes per side, or until an instant-read thermometer registers 170°F (80°C).

YIELD: 3–4 servings

Assuming 3 servings, each will have 2 grams of carbohydrate and 1 gram of fiber, for a usable carb count of 1 gram; 35 grams protein.

chapter four

Chicken, Turkey, and Other Birds

Chicken is second only to pork as America's favorite meat to barbecue, and for good reason—it's delicious. It's also generally cheaper than pork, and it doesn't run afoul of most common dietary taboos. You can see why we throw chicken on the grill on a regular basis!

But other birds are great grilled or smoked, too. Turkey responds very well to barbecuing, and the proliferation of turkey parts in grocery stores means you don't have to take the time to smoke a whole darned bird to have great barbecued turkey—you can smoke just a turkey breast, or barbecue a chorus line of drumsticks.

You'll find duck and Cornish game hens here, too! So, grab some birds and fire up the grill!

☀ Absolutely Classic Barbecued Chicken

You'll notice that this is remarkably similar to the Absolutely Classic Barbecued Ribs, the only difference being that it's chicken!

> 3 pounds (1.5 kilograms) cut-up chicken (on the bone, skin on—choose light or dark meat, as you prefer)
> 1/3 cup (40 grams) Classic Barbecue Rub (page 31)
> 1/2 cup (120 milliliters) chicken broth
> 1/2 cup (120 milliliters) oil
> 1/2 cup (120 grams) Kansas City Barbecue Sauce (page 32)

Get your fire going, with your grill set up for indirect smoking.

While the grill's heating, sprinkle the chicken with all but a tablespoon of the rub. Combine the reserved rub with the chicken broth and oil, to make a mop.

When your fire is ready, place your chicken over a drip pan, add your chips or chunks, and close the grill. Let it smoke for half an hour before you start to baste it with the mop, then mop it every time you add more chips or chunks. Smoke your chicken for about 90 minutes, or until an instant-read thermometer registers 180°F (85°C). When your chicken is just about done, baste the skin side with the Kansas City Barbecue Sauce and move it over the fire, skin-side down for 5 minutes or so. Baste the other side with the finishing sauce, turn it over, and give it another 5 minutes over the fire. Serve with the rest of the sauce.

Feel free to use this same basic method with any rub and any sauce!

YIELD: 5 servings

Each serving will have 9 grams of carbohydrate and 1 gram of fiber, for a usable carb count of 8 grams; 35 grams protein.

✺ Orange-Tangerine Up-the-Butt Chicken

Once someone figured out that standing a chicken up on a beer can made for a perfectly roasted chicken, soda-can chicken was inevitable!

 1 3 1/2–4-pound (2-kilogram) whole roasting chicken

 1 teaspoon salt or Vege-Sal

 1 teaspoon Splenda

 1 drop blackstrap molasses (It helps to keep your molasses in
    a squeeze bottle.)

 1 teaspoon chili powder

 3 tablespoons low-sugar orange marmalade

 1 12-ounce (360-milliliter) can tangerine Diet-Rite soda, divided
    (Make sure the can is clean!)

 2–3 teaspoons oil

 1 teaspoon spicy brown mustard

Prepare your grill for indirect cooking—if you have a gas grill, light only one side; if you're using charcoal, pile the briquettes on one side of the grill, and light.

Remove the neck and giblets from the chicken (if you have a dog, it'll be very happy to eat the giblets for you!). Rinse your chicken and pat it dry with paper towels.

In a small bowl combine the salt or Vege-Sal, Splenda, molasses, and chili powder. Spoon out half the mixture (1 1/2 teaspoons) into a bowl and reserve; rub the rest inside the cavity of your chicken.

Stir the low-sugar orange marmalade into the reserved seasoning mixture. Open the can of tangerine soda, and pour out 2/3 of a cup. Put 1/4 of a cup of the soda you poured off into the marmalade/seasoning mixture, and stir it in—you can drink the remainder of the soda you poured off, or throw it away. Now, using a church-key type can opener, punch several more holes around the top of the can. Spray the can with nonstick cooking spray, and set it in a shallow baking pan. Carefully place your chicken down over the can, fitting the can up into the cavity of the chicken. Rub your chicken with the oil.

Okay, you're ready to cook! Make sure you have a drip pan in place. Set your chicken, standing upright on its soda can, on the side of the grill not over the fire, and spread the drumsticks out a bit, making a tripod effect. Close the grill, and cook your chicken at 250°F (130°C) or so for 75–90 minutes, or until the juices run clear when it's pricked to the bone. You can also use a meat thermometer—it should register 180°F (85°C).

While your chicken is roasting, add the mustard to the marmalade/soda/seasoning mixture, and stir the whole thing up. Use this mixture to baste the chicken during the last 20 minutes or so of roasting.

When the chicken is done, carefully remove it from the grill—barbecue gloves come in handy here, or use heavy hot pads and tongs. Twist the can to remove it from the chicken, and discard. Let the chicken stand for 5 minutes before carving. In the meanwhile, heat any leftover basting sauce to boiling—even though it shouldn't have any chicken germs, having been used only after the chicken was well heated, who wants to take chances?—and serve as a sauce with the chicken.

YIELD: 5 servings

Each serving will have 5 grams of carbohydrate and a trace of fiber. Assuming a 3 1/2-pound chicken, each serving will have 40 grams of protein.

☀ Alabama Amber Glow Chicken

White barbecue sauce—mayonnaise based and nothing like the stuff in bottles at the grocery store—is an Alabama specialty. After long, slow smoking, the chicken turns a rich amber color and has a wonderfully mellow flavor.

> 1 batch Alabama White Sauce (page 43)
> 3–3 1/2 pounds (1.5 kilograms) cut-up chicken

Set up your grill for indirect smoking, as described in chapter 1.

Set aside half of your Alabama White Sauce—about 1/3 cup—to use as a finishing sauce. Slow smoke your chicken for a good 2 hours, brushing lightly with the sauce now and then. You'll want to smoke it until the juices run clear when it's pierced to the bone and/or an instant-read thermometer registers 180°F (85°C).

Spoon a tablespoon of the reserved sauce over each serving.

YIELD: 6 servings

Each serving will have 1 gram of carbohydrate, a trace of fiber, and 29 grams protein.

☀ Orange Blossom Turkey Breast

This is very moist and tasty! Wonderful left over, too, especially made into turkey salad.

> 1/2 cup (120 milliliters) white wine vinegar
>
> 1/2 teaspoon orange extract
>
> 1/4 cup (85 grams) sugar-free imitation honey
>
> 1/4 cup (60 milliliters) Splenda
>
> 1/4 cup (60 grams) yellow mustard
>
> 2 tablespoons soy sauce
>
> 3 cloves garlic
>
> 1 turkey breast, bone in, about 5 pounds (2.5 kilograms)

For this recipe, it's really nice to have a meat injector—basically a big hypodermic syringe used for injecting meat with various flavors. They're pretty easy to find, and even easier to use! If you don't have one, this is still a great marinade, but it won't penetrate the meat quite so much.

Mix together everything but the turkey breast. Put the breast in a nonreactive bowl that's fairly deep and narrow, and pour the marinade over it. Stick the whole thing in the fridge, and let the breast marinate all day, or even overnight, turning it now and then. If you have a meat injector, suck up some marinade with it, and inject the breast all over with the marinade.

When the time comes to cook, set up your grill for indirect cooking—pile the charcoal to the side, or light only one gas burner. Have plenty of wood chips soaking! Place a drip pan under the grill under where you're placing the turkey, and put the turkey on the grill. Smoke the turkey according to the directions in chapter 1 for about 1 3/4–2 hours, replacing the wood chips whenever the smoke stops, maintaining the grill temperature at about 225°F (110°C). Baste the turkey now and then with the marinade, but stop a good half hour before the end of cooking time, to make sure all the germs are dead. The turkey is done when a meat thermometer stuck in the thickest part of the breast (but not touching the bone) registers 170°F (80°C). Remove from the grill, and let the breast sit for 10 minutes before carving.

YIELD: 8–10 servings

Assuming 8 servings, each would have 9 grams of carbohydrate (not counting the polyols in the imitation honey) if you ate all of the marinade. Since you won't, figure closer to 4 or 5 grams per serving; 57 grams of protein.

☀ Mediterranean Marinated Turkey Legs

Turkey legs are a convenient cut to grill or barbecue—they cook relatively quickly and are a nice one-serving size. Oh, and they taste great, too!

> 3 turkey legs
>
> 1/2 cup (120 milliliters) olive oil
>
> 1/3 cup (80 milliliters) red wine vinegar
>
> 3 cloves garlic
>
> 1 tablespoon lemon juice

Put your turkey legs in a big zipper-lock bag. Mix everything else together, pour into the bag, press the air out of the bag, and turn the bag a few times to coat. Stash in the fridge, and let your turkey legs marinate for several hours.

Okay, cooking time! Get a fire going; you'll want a medium fire. Pour the marinade off into a dish, and reserve. Smoke the legs over indirect heat in a closed grill, following the instructions in chapter 1. Baste every 15 minutes or so with the marinade, and turn, then close the grill again. They'll take about an hour.

YIELD: 3 servings, 1 leg per customer

Even If you drank the leftover marinade (which you won't! Germs!) you'd get only 3 grams of carbohydrate per serving, with a trace of fiber. As it is, I'd count no more than 2 grams, and maybe 1. About 47 grams of protein—it depends on the size of your legs!

✺ Tequila Citrus Game Hens

1/2 cup (120 milliliters) lime juice

1/2 cup (120 milliliters) lemon juice

1/4 teaspoon orange extract

1 tablespoon Splenda

1 cup (225 milliliters) tequila

1/4 medium onion, minced fine

1/4 cup (60 milliliters) olive oil

2 tablespoons Worcestershire sauce

1 whole jalapeno, seeded and minced fine

2 Cornish game hens

I like to put everything but the hens in a blender, and whiz everything up (and don't forget to wash your hands after handling that jalapeno!). Put the hens in a nonreactive container just big enough to hold them. Pour the marinade over the hens, turn them once or twice to make sure that the hens are coated, and make sure some marinade gets inside the body cavities. Stick the whole thing in the fridge for at least 3 or 4 hours, and all day won't hurt a bit.

A couple of hours before dinnertime, get the grill going. Smoke according to the directions for indirect cooking in chapter 1, basting every 30 minutes or so with the marinade, for about 2 1/2 hours or until their leg joints move freely. An instant-read thermometer inserted into the thickest part of the meat (but not touching the bone) should register 180°F–185°F (85°C). Remove the birds from the grill and allow them to sit for 5–10 minutes before carving.

While those birds are resting, bring the marinade to a boil, and boil it hard for at least 3 or 4 minutes. Thicken it a little with your guar or xanthan shaker, if you like, and serve as a sauce with the hens.

YIELD: This is 2 hefty but elegant whole-bird servings, or 4 more reasonable but less picturesque servings.

Assuming 2 servings, you'll get 16 grams of carbohydrate and 1 gram of fiber— if you eat all of the marinade, so don't eat all of the marinade! Just have a spoonful or two, and you can figure on getting 2 or 3 grams of usable carb; 59 grams of protein.

About Grilling Chicken on the Bone

Boneless, skinless chicken breast has nearly taken over the market, yet chicken cooked with the skin and on the bone is far, far juicier and more flavorful, and while it takes a little longer to cook, it's hardly terribly time-consuming. Anyway, I like dark meat best.

One piece of information I'd like to pass on to you: In grilling a copious quantity of chicken in the writing of this cookbook, I learned that the chicken cooked quicker, and with the fewest flare-ups, if I kept the grill hood down except while basting or turning my chicken, or, indeed, keeping down flare-ups with a squirt bottle of water. This, however, leads to the interesting question of how one knows that the fire is flaring up if the hood is closed?

The answer is that you listen, and from time to time you check, re-closing the lid after checking and squirting if necessary.

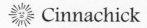 Cinnachick

Really unusual, and wonderful!

 ½ cup (120 milliliters) dry sherry

 3 tablespoons sugar-free imitation honey

 3 tablespoons Splenda

 2 teaspoons ground cinnamon

 1 teaspoon curry powder

 1 clove garlic, crushed

 ½ teaspoon salt

 1 broiler-fryer, cut up—about 2 ½–3 pounds (1.5 kilograms)

Just combine everything but the chicken and pour it over your chicken in a shallow, nonreactive pan or a zipper-lock bag. If you're using a bag, press out the air and seal it. Put your chicken in the fridge, and let it marinate for anywhere from a few hours to all day.

Then heat your grill—medium-high for a gas grill, or well-ashed coals in a charcoal grill. Grill your chicken bone-side down for about 12 minutes, then turn it and grill it for 7 or 8 minutes skin-side down. Keep the hood closed except when turning the chicken, or fighting off flare-ups with your squirt bottle. Turn it again, and grill until juices run clear when the chicken is pierced to the bone. Baste chicken frequently with the marinade, but stop basting a good 5 minutes before the chicken is done, to make sure all the raw chicken germs are killed by the heat.

YIELD: 4 servings

4 grams of carbohydrate, not counting the polyols in the imitation honey; 1 gram fiber. These figures, however, assume you'll consume all of the marinade, which you won't—so I'd guess no more than 2 grams per serving; 36 grams of protein.

Balsamic-Mustard Chicken

1 broiler-fryer chicken, about 3 pounds (1.5 kilograms), cut up, or whatever
  chicken parts you like

2 tablespoons chili garlic paste

1/2 cup (125 grams) spicy brown mustard

1/4 cup (60 milliliters) balsamic vinegar

1/4 cup (60 milliliters) olive oil

Put your chicken parts in a large, heavy zipper-lock bag. Combine everything else and whisk together well, then pour into the bag with the chicken, press out the air, and seal the bag. Throw the bag in the fridge, and let your chicken marinate for anywhere from a few hours to all day.

When it's time to cook, light your charcoal or gas grill; you'll want a medium to medium-high fire. When the grill is ready, pull the chicken out of the marinade using tongs, and place it on a plate. Pour the marinade into a bowl, for basting.

Now put your chicken on the grill skin-side up, and grill it for 12–15 minutes. Turn it, and let it grill for 7–9 minutes skin-side down. Turn it again, and cook for another 5–10 minutes or until the juices run clear when it's pierced to the bone and an instant-read thermometer reads 180°F (85°C). Baste frequently with the marinade, finishing basting with at least 5 minutes of cooking time to go. Keep the grill closed except when basting or turning the chicken.

YIELD: 5–6 servings

Assuming 6 servings, if you ate/drank all the marinade, each would have 3 grams of carbohydrate and a trace of fiber, but actually you'll get less than that. Assuming 6 servings, each will have 30 grams of protein.

☀ Chili-Lime Chicken

This was a big hit at our annual Toastmasters Bash at the Lake.

> 3 pounds (1.5 kilograms) chicken pieces—either a cut-up broiler/fryer
>   or whatever parts you like (I used thighs)
> 1 tablespoon chili garlic paste
> 2 cloves garlic, crushed
> 1 tablespoon grated gingerroot
> 1/4 cup (60 milliliters) soy sauce
> 1/2 cup (120 milliliters) lime juice
> 3 tablespoons Splenda

Plunk your chicken into a big zipper-lock bag. Mix together everything else, pour it into the bag with the chicken, press out the air, and seal the bag. Throw the bag in the fridge, and let your chicken marinate for at least a few hours, more won't hurt.

When it's time to cook, fire up the grill—you'll want medium to medium-high heat. Just drain the marinade off the chicken and throw it on the grill skin-side up when it's ready. Close the grill, and keep it closed until it's time to turn the chicken, unless you suspect a flare-up. Cook for about 12–15 minutes, turn skin-side down and give it another 7–9 minutes, then turn skin-side up again and let it cook until the juices run clear when it's pierced to the bone and an instant-read thermometer registers 180°F (85°C). Then serve!

YIELD: 6 servings

If you drank the marinade (don't you dare!), you'd get 5 grams of carb and a trace of fiber per serving, but since you discard most of it, you won't get anywhere near that much—I'd count no more than 1–2 grams per serving. Assuming 6 servings, each will have 30 grams of protein.

☀ Drunken Chicken Wings

I'd call these Chinese-inspired, except for the bourbon, which is all-American. How about East-Meets-West?

20 whole chicken wings, or 40 drummettes

1 tablespoon fish sauce (nuoc mam or nam pla)

1 tablespoon grated gingerroot

2 teaspoons black pepper

1 teaspoon chili garlic paste

1/4 cup (60 milliliters) Splenda

2 tablespoons sugar-free imitation honey

1/4 cup (60 milliliters) bourbon

Throw your wings into a large zipper-lock plastic bag. Mix together everything else, and pour over the wings. Press out the air, seal the bag, and toss it in the fridge. Let your wings live it up for at least a few hours.

When it's time to cook, light your grill; you'll want it medium-high. When the fire is ready, pour the marinade off into a bowl, and arrange the wings on the grill. Grill for 7–10 minutes per side, basting often with the marinade—but be careful to do your last basting with at least five minutes of cooking time to go. Discard the rest of the marinade, and serve your wings!

YIELD: You will, of course, have 20 wings or 40 drummettes—how many servings will depend on whether you're serving these as a main dish or an appetizer.

Whichever, each whole wing will have well under 1 gram of usable carbohydrate, and 9 grams of protein. Halve those figures for drummettes.

☀ Korean Barbecued Chicken

Hot, spicy, garlicky, and a little sweet, this is truly wonderful. And unlike classic American barbecued chicken, this is actually grilled, so it cooks faster than the slow-smoked variety.

2 pounds (1 kilogram) chicken pieces

2 tablespoons chili garlic paste

3 tablespoons dry sherry

1 tablespoon soy sauce

4 cloves garlic, crushed

1 1/2 tablespoons toasted sesame oil

1 tablespoon grated gingerroot

2 scallions, minced

2 teaspoons black pepper

1 tablespoon Splenda

Put your chicken in a large zipper-lock plastic bag. Mix together everything else, and pour it over the chicken. Press out the air, seal the bag, and toss it in the fridge. Let your chicken marinate for several hours.

When it's time to cook, fire up the grill. You'll want it at medium to medium-high. When the grill is ready for cooking, remove the chicken from the bag, and pour the marinade into a bowl for basting. Cook your chicken skin-side up for about 12–15 minutes, keeping the grill closed except when basting. Turn it skin-side down and let it grill for 7–9 minutes, again with the grill closed. Turn it skin-side up again, and let it grill until the juices run clear when pierced to the bone and an instant-read thermometer registers 180°F (85°C). Baste several times with the marinade while cooking, basting for the last time at least 5 minutes before you're done cooking the chicken. Discard remaining marinade, and serve chicken.

YIELD: 4 servings

With all the marinade, each serving would have 4 grams of carbohydrate and 1 gram of fiber, but you won't consume all the marinade; I'd count no more than 3 grams per serving; 30 grams of protein.

 # San Diego Chicken

A version of this recipe appeared in my local paper, and though it looked tasty, it was way too high-carb for us. I played around with it, cut out a lot of the carbs, and ended up with this recipe—fruity and tomatoey and yummy.

    1 8-ounce (230-gram) can tomato sauce

    1 tablespoon lemon juice

    1 tablespoon lime juice

    1/8 teaspoon lemon extract

    1/2 teaspoon orange extract

    3 tablespoons Splenda

    3 tablespoons white wine vinegar (if you don't have any on hand,
        I'm sure cider vinegar would taste fine—different, but fine)

    2 cloves garlic, crushed

    1 teaspoon Italian seasoning

    1 teaspoon hot sauce

    3 pounds (1.5 kilograms) cut-up chicken

Mix together everything but the chicken pieces. Place the chicken pieces in a large zipper-lock bag, and pour the tomato sauce mixture over it. Seal the bag, pressing out the air as you go, and turn to coat all the chicken pieces. Let your chicken marinate for at least a few hours, and I'm betting a day wouldn't hurt a bit.

When you're ready to cook: Get your grill ready—charcoal covered with white ash, or gas grill set to medium. Pull your chicken out of the marinade and pour the marinade out of the bag, into a saucepan. Go throw your chicken on the grill, bone-side down; close the lid; and set a timer for 13–15 minutes.

While the chicken is grilling, put that pan of marinade over a low burner, and let it come to a simmer. Now, go check your chicken for flare-ups—I keep a squeeze bottle of water by the grill to keep these at bay. You want your chicken cooked, not charred!

Timer gone ding? Turn your chicken, using a pair of tongs. Set your timer for another 13–15 minutes. When time's up, turn it skin-side up again, and pierce a piece to the bone, to make sure all the juices are running clear. If there's any pink in the juices, let your chicken cook another few minutes.

When it's done, serve each piece with a little of that marinade you simmered spooned over the top. Enjoy!

> **Note:** I use serious Jamaican scotch bonnet hot sauce in this, and it isn't scorch your mouth hot, just nicely spicy. If you want to, you can crank the heat up or down by either using more or less hot sauce or using hotter or less-hot sauce.

YIELD: 6 servings

Each serving will have 5 grams of carbohydrate and 1 gram of fiber, for a usable carb count of 4 grams; 29 grams of protein.

 ## Chicken Adobo

Simple and Southwestern.

> 3–3 1/2 pounds (1.5 kilograms) cut-up chicken
> 1 batch Adobo Sauce (page 60)

Put your chicken in a big zipper-lock bag and pour the Adobo Sauce over it. Press the air out of the bag, seal it, turn it over a few times to make sure the chicken is coated, and throw it in the fridge. Let it marinate at least 8–10 hours, and a whole day would be great.

Okay, get your grill going—you'll want a medium fire. Pull your chicken out of the fridge, remove it from the bag, and drain off the marinade into a bowl. Cook your chicken skin-side up for about 12–15 minutes, keeping the grill closed except when basting. Turn it skin-side down, and let it grill for 7–9 minutes, again with the grill closed. Turn it skin-side up again, and let it grill until the juices run clear when pierced to the bone and an instant-read thermometer registers 180°F (85°C). Baste several times with the marinade while cooking, basting for the last time at least 5 minutes before you're done cooking the chicken. Discard remaining marinade, and serve chicken.

YIELD: About 5 servings

If you consumed all the marinade, this would have 5 grams of carbohydrate with a trace of fiber per serving, but you won't consume all the marinade—say no more than 3 grams of carb per serving; 34 grams of protein.

☀ Grilled Curried Chicken with Apricot Sauce

The curry and apricot really sing together!

>3 pounds (1.5 kilograms) cut-up chicken
>
>1/4 cup (30 grams) Curry Rub (page 70)
>
>1/2 cup (120 grams) Apricot White Wine Sauce (page 65)

Have your grill going first; you'll want a medium fire.

Sprinkle your chicken all over with the Curry Rub, then throw it on the grill, skin-side up. Cook your chicken skin-side up for about 12–15 minutes, keeping the grill closed except if you need to combat flare-ups. Turn it skin-side down, and let it grill for 7–9 minutes, again with the grill closed. Turn it skin-side up again, and let it grill until the juices run clear when pierced to the bone and an instant-read thermometer registers 180°F (85°C). Brush the skin side lightly with a little of the Apricot White Wine Sauce, close the grill, and give it just a few more minutes, to glaze the chicken. Serve with the rest of the sauce spooned over it.

YIELD: About 5 servings

Each serving will have 6 grams of carbohydrate and 1 gram of fiber, for a usable carb count of 5 grams; 35 grams protein.

☀ Spatchcocked (or UnSpatchcocked) Chicken with Vinegar Baste

Treating chicken to an acidic baste or marinade of some kind is a time-honored way of bringing out the flavor of our favorite fowl. This baste also adds some heat and complex spiciness—yum! What the heck is "spatchcocked" chicken? It's a chicken that's been cut along the backbone and opened up flat, for easier grilling.

>3 1/2 pounds (1.5 kilograms) chicken—either whole or cut up
>
>1 cup (225 milliliters) cider vinegar
>
>3 teaspoons chili powder
>
>2 tablespoons Splenda
>
>1 teaspoon cayenne

1 teaspoon paprika

1 teaspoon dry mustard

1 teaspoon black pepper

1/2 teaspoon cumin

1/2 teaspoon salt

Technically, you're supposed to cut along both sides of the backbone and remove it entirely, but that's too much work for me, so I just let my chicken look uneven. I know this sounds hard, but if you have good poultry or kitchen shears—my Martha Stewart shears from Kmart work just fine—it takes all of about a minute and a half. Make the cut along the bottom side of the chicken, grab either side of the cut, and pull the chicken open. Press down on the breastbone until you hear a slight crack, to flatten the bird. Now you have a flat chicken you can lay on a grill.

Or you can just not bother. I'm describing the process because it's terribly, terribly trendy in grilling circles right now, and anyway, whole chickens are often quite cheap. However, I think it's easier just to use a cut-up chicken, you know? The baste works just as well with the parts, and you don't have to carve.

Either way, start by lighting your grill; you'll want it at medium heat. While the grill is heating, combine everything but the chicken.

Grill your chicken starting skin-side up, and, keeping the grill closed except when basting or dealing with flare-ups, grill for 15 minutes, basting frequently with the vinegar mixture. Turn skin-side down and grill for 7–9 minutes, still basting; then turn skin-side up again and continue grilling until juices run clear when chicken is pierced to the bone or an instant-read thermometer registers 180°F (85°C). Serve.

YIELD: 5 servings

Even with all of the basting liquid you'd get only 5 grams of carb, with 1 gram of fiber, or 4 grams of usable carb per serving—but you won't consume all of the basting liquid. Count no more than 2 grams per serving; 40 grams of protein.

Sherry-Mustard-Soy Marinated Chicken

¼ cup (60 milliliters) Splenda

3 tablespoons olive oil

3 tablespoons sherry

1 tablespoon mustard

1 tablespoon soy sauce

1 tablespoon black pepper

½ tablespoon Worcestershire sauce

¼ cup (40 grams) minced onion

1 clove garlic, crushed

2 tablespoons water

3 ½–4 pounds (2 kilograms) cut-up chicken

Combine everything but the chicken, mixing well. Put your chicken either in a shallow, nonreactive pan or in a large zipper-lock bag. Either way, pour the marinade over the chicken. If it's in a pan, turn it once or twice to coat. If it's in a bag, press out the air, seal the bag, and turn it a few times to coat the chicken. Either way, stick your chicken in the fridge, and let it marinate for at least 1 or 2 hours, and longer won't hurt.

When the chicken is ready to grill, have the gas grill set to medium, or the charcoal covered with white ash. Grill the chicken bone-side down for 10–12 minutes with the lid closed (but check now and then for flare-ups!), basting with the marinade once or twice. Turn the chicken over with tongs and grill skin-side down for 6–7 minutes, again with the grill closed, but check now and then for flare-ups. Turn the chicken back to bone-side down, baste it one more time, and grill with the lid closed for another 5–10 minutes, until the juices run clear when the chicken is pierced to the bone or until an instant-read thermometer reads 180°F (85°C).

YIELD: 5–6 servings

Assuming 6, and assuming you consumed all the marinade, each serving would have 4 grams of carb and 1 gram of fiber, for a usable carb count of 3 grams. Since you won't consume all of the marinade, however, I'd count 2 grams per serving; 34 grams protein.

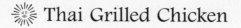# Thai Grilled Chicken

1/4 cup (60 milliliters) coconut milk (find this in cans at Asian markets
   or in grocery stores with a good international section)

2 tablespoons fish sauce (nuoc mam or nam pla)

2 tablespoons lime juice

2 teaspoons Splenda

2 cloves garlic

1/2 teaspoon turmeric

1 1/2 pounds (700 grams) boneless, skinless chicken breast

Combine everything but the chicken, and stir well. Pour over the chicken in a large zipper-lock bag. Press out the air, seal the bag, and toss it in the fridge for 1 or 2 hours, and all day won't hurt.

When dinnertime rolls around, light your grill. When the grill is hot, cook the chicken for about 7 minutes per side, or until done through. Serve with Thai Peanut Sauce (page 118).

YIELD: 5 servings

Each serving will have no more than 3 grams of carbohydrate before adding the peanut sauce—and once again, actually a bit less because of the marinade that gets thrown away—31 grams of protein. Analysis does not include the Thai Peanut Sauce.

☀ Thai Peanut Sauce

1/2 teaspoon hot sauce

1 tablespoon grated gingerroot

1 clove garlic, crushed

2 scallions, sliced, including the crisp part of the green

1/3 cup (80 grams) natural peanut butter

1/3 cup (80 milliliters) coconut milk (find this in cans in Asian markets
 or grocery stores with good international sections)

2 tablespoons fish sauce (nam pla or nuoc mam)

1 1/2 tablespoons lime juice

2 teaspoons Splenda

Put everything in your blender, or in your food processor with the S-blade in place, and process until smooth. Serve with Thai Grilled Chicken (page 117).

YIELD: Makes roughly a cup, or 8 servings of 2 tablespoons each

4 grams of carbohydrate per serving, and 1 gram of fiber, for a usable carb count of 3 grams; 3 grams of protein.

☀ Sweet Lemon-Brined and Glazed Chicken Breast

Like the convenience of boneless, skinless chicken breasts but find they often come out bland and dry? With this recipe, they'll be plump, moist, and flavorful, even if you overcook them a little!

1 1/2 pounds (700 grams) boneless, skinless chicken breast

Brine:

16 ounces (480 milliliters) lemon-flavored Fruit$_2$O

1 tablespoon kosher salt

1 tablespoon soy sauce

1 clove garlic

1 dash Tabasco sauce

Glaze:

2 tablespoons lemon juice

1 tablespoon DiabetiSweet or other polyol-based sweetener

1/2 tablespoon soy sauce

1 clove garlic

Cut your chicken breasts into 4 portions if needed.

Dissolve the salt in the Fruit$_2$O. (Heating the Fruit$_2$O will help the salt dissolve.) Then stir in the rest of the brine ingredients. Pour over the chicken breasts in a shallow, nonreactive dish small enough that the breasts are submerged, and stick the whole thing in the fridge.

Three to 4 hours later, get your grill going. When the coals are well ashed, or the gas grill is heated to medium, pull the chicken out of the fridge and drain off the brine. Make sure your grill is well oiled, then grill the chicken about 7–10 minutes per side or until an instant-read thermometer registers 180°F (85°C).

While the chicken is grilling, combine the glaze ingredients in a small saucepan and simmer for just 1–2 minutes. Brush over the chicken during the last few minutes of grilling. If there's any glaze left over, drizzle it over the chicken before serving.

YIELD: 4 servings

Each serving will have 2 grams carbohydrate, a trace of fiber, and 38 grams protein.

☀ Apricot-Rosemary Glazed Chicken Breasts

Very speedy, especially if you have a gas grill, and very good!

> 2 tablespoons low-sugar apricot preserves
>
> 2 teaspoons ground rosemary
>
> 2 teaspoons lemon juice
>
> 2 cloves garlic, crushed
>
> 4 boneless, skinless chicken breasts—1 1/2 –2 pounds (1 kilogram) total

First, light your charcoal or start heating your gas grill. You'll want medium heat.

Simply combine everything but the chicken breasts in a bowl, and mix well. Cut your chicken breasts into serving-sized portions if needed. Start the chicken breasts grilling over medium heat, brushing the side that's up with apricot mixture. After about 7 minutes, brush with apricot mixture again, turn, and brush with the glaze again. Grill another 7 minutes or so, brushing a couple of times with the apricot glaze, but stop basting with a few minutes of cooking time to go, so as not to reintroduce raw chicken germs to your dinner!

When the breasts are done through, serve. If there's any apricot glaze remaining, you can heat it thoroughly in the microwave—make sure it boils hard!—and spoon it over the breasts before serving.

YIELD: 4 servings

Each serving will have 4 grams of carbohydrate and a trace of fiber. Assuming 1 1/2 pounds of chicken, each serving will have 38 grams of protein.

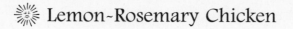 Lemon-Rosemary Chicken

Okay, this bears a certain resemblance to the previous recipe. It actually tastes quite different, though. This is a very classic flavor combination.

1/4 cup (60 milliliters) olive oil

2 tablespoons lemon juice

2 cloves garlic, crushed

1 tablespoon dried rosemary, crushed a bit

1 pound (500 grams) boneless, skinless chicken breast

Mix together everything but the chicken. Put the chicken breasts in a shallow dish, and pour the olive oil/lemon mixture over the chicken. Turn the breasts over once or twice to coat them. (We're not doing this in a bag, because we're going to marinate the chicken for only a short time.)

Now, go start your grill. You'll want it at medium heat. When it's ready, throw the chicken on the grill, and cook for about 7 minutes per side, basting with the olive oil/lemon mixture a few times. As always, baste for the last time when you still have at least 5 minutes of cooking time left, to make sure you kill the raw chicken germs!

I like to heat the marinade till it boils hard, and then spoon just a little over each breast while serving.

YIELD: 3 servings

Even if you consumed all the marinade, which you won't, you'd get only 2 grams of carb per serving, 1 gram of which would be fiber. 34 grams protein.

☀ Sesame Orange Duck

Duck is unbelievably rich—but what a special-occasion treat! If you'd like, you can cook chicken the same way, for a less-expensive, lower-calorie dish.

4 tablespoons soy sauce

2 tablespoons low-sugar orange marmalade

1/4 teaspoon orange extract

2 teaspoons Splenda

2 cloves garlic

2 teaspoons grated gingerroot

2 tablespoons white wine vinegar

1 duck, cut into 4 servings

4 tablespoons sesame seeds

Before we get to the recipe, let's talk about cutting up the duck. My grocery store didn't have duck in stock, so I asked them to order a couple for me. They came in whole and frozen. I let my duck thaw, and it then took me about 5 minutes to cut it up using my trusty Kmart shears—not a big deal. However, if you'd prefer, you could ask the nice meat guys at your grocery store if they could order you a cut-up duck, or, alternately, let the duck thaw there and cut it up for you. If you choose this last option, however, don't take your duck home and refreeze it—just arrange for it to be ready to pick up the day you want to cook it.

Okay, to cook your duck! Mix together the soy sauce, orange marmalade, orange extract, Splenda, garlic, ginger, and vinegar in a bowl. Tear off 4 sheets of heavy-duty aluminum foil, each big enough to wrap one of your pieces of duck. Put a piece of duck on a piece of foil and bend up the edges enough that the sauce won't run off. Spoon about 1 tablespoon of sauce over the piece of duck, smear it around a little with the back of the spoon, and wrap the piece of duck—fold opposite edges to the middle, roll down, then roll the ends in. Repeat with the remaining 3 pieces of duck and pieces of foil.

Grill your duck packets over a medium fire for about 40 minutes, turning halfway through.

In the meanwhile, toast your sesame seeds by putting them in a small, dry skillet and shaking them over a hot burner until they start to make little popping sounds. Turn off the burner, and if you have an electric stove, remove the skillet from the burner so the residual heat doesn't burn the seeds.

Okay, 40 minutes is up. Retrieve the duck from the grill and carefully unwrap each piece. Put the unwrapped duck back on the grill, skin-side down, for 5 minutes, or until the skin is crisp. Remove to serving plates, top each with 1/2 tablespoon of sesame seeds, and serve.

YIELD: 4 servings

Each serving will have 4 grams of carbohydrate and 1 gram of fiber, for a usable carb count of 3 grams; 39 grams of protein.

chapter five

Beef and Lamb

Only ever barbecued pork and chicken? You're missing something! Beef and lamb both respond marvelously to the slow smoke treatment. Indeed, in Texas—you know, cattle country—beef is the favorite meat to barbecue. Give it a try!

Everybody loves grilling beef—what's more popular than charcoal-grilled steak and flame-broiled burgers? You'll find some new ways with both in this chapter, not that there's anything wrong with just plain grilled steak, thank you very much. Still, sometimes you want something new and different, not to mention yummy—so here it is!

☀ Lone Star Brisket

Here's the Texan's take on barbecue. Makes a really tasty morsel out of a tough, inexpensive brisket! The Texas BBQ Brisket Sauce on page 52 would be a natural with this.

> 2 pounds (1 kilogram) beef brisket
>
> 1 teaspoon meat tenderizer
>
> 1/2 cup (120 milliliters) oil
>
> 1/2 cup (120 milliliters) cider vinegar
>
> 1 teaspoon chili powder
>
> 2 tablespoons Worcestershire sauce
>
> 1 teaspoon Splenda
>
> 1/2 teaspoon pepper

Sprinkle one side of your brisket with 1/2 teaspoon of the tenderizer, and pierce the meat all over with a fork. Turn it over, and treat the other side the same way. Put the brisket in a shallow, nonreactive pan.

Mix together the remaining ingredients, pour over the brisket, and turn it once or twice to coat. Let the brisket marinate for several hours, at least, and overnight is great.

At least 3 hours before dinner, set up your grill for indirect cooking as described in chapter 1. Smoke the brisket for about 3 hours or until tender, mopping with the marinade every half hour or so.

YIELD: 5–6 servings

Assuming 6, each would have 3 grams of carbohydrate if you ate all the marinade—which you won't. Figure that you'll get no more than 1 gram of carb per serving, not including any finishing sauce you might add; 26 grams of protein.

☀ Bodacious Brined and Barbecued Beef Brisket

Stand back when you say that! Most Americans have tried one form of brined brisket—corned beef. Well, this may be a brined brisket, but it ain't much like corned beef—hot and spicy and so yummy that adding sauce would be a sin. Eat it as is!

2 pounds (1 kilogram) beef brisket

2 teaspoons meat tenderizer

1 quart (1 liter) water

2 tablespoons kosher salt

1 tablespoon chili powder

2 tablespoons Splenda

2 cloves garlic

1 tablespoon tomato paste

Bodacious Beef Brisket Rub (page 46)

Bodacious Beef Brisket Beer Mop (page 47)

Put your brisket on a plate, sprinkle one side with 1 teaspoon of the meat tenderizer, and pierce it all over with a fork. Flip 'er over and do the same to the other side, with the remaining teaspoon of tenderizer. Let that sit a minute.

In a flat, shallow, nonreactive container just big enough to hold your hunk of brisket, dissolve the salt in the water (using warm water helps). Stir in the chili powder, Splenda, garlic, and tomato paste. Submerge your brisket in the brine—add just a little more water if your brisket isn't totally submerged. Let your brisket brine for 3–5 hours.

When brining time is up, pull out your brisket and sprinkle it liberally all over with the Bodacious Beef Brisket Rub. Set up your grill for indirect cooking, and smoke your brisket for a good 3–4 hours. Mop with the Bodacious Beef Brisket Beer Mop every half hour to 45 minutes.

When smoking time's up, slice your brisket thin across the grain, and serve.

YIELD: Figure 6 servings

This was one of the hardest recipes to estimate the correct carb count for. The analysis comes up saying 19 grams of carbohydrate per serving, with 3 grams of fiber, but the vast majority of that is in the brine and the mop. I'm going to say about 6 grams of carb per serving, and I think that's actually high; 28 grams of protein.

About Beef Ribs

Before I started writing this book, neither my husband nor I had ever had a beef spare rib. Now they're one of our favorites! Beef ribs are less meaty than pork ribs, so there are fewer servings to a slab—figure 1 slab of about 2 1/2–3 pounds will feed three to four people.

Before you get around to seasoning your beef ribs, you need to remove the heavy membrane on the back. This will take a sharp knife and some tough talk, but it will leave your ribs far more easily eat-able. By the way, if you have dogs, save the membranes for them, and they'll be even more devoted to you than they already are. My dogs, Jed and Molly, were crazy about the stuff.

Around here—Southern Indiana—racks of beef ribs show up in the grocery store only sporadically, so when I see them, I grab several and stash them in the freezer. If you don't find them in your grocery store, ask the nice meat guys if they can order them for you. In my experience, the meat guys are very helpful.

⁂ Lone Star Beef Ribs

1 rack beef ribs, about 2 1/2–3 pounds (1.5 kilograms)

1/3 cup (40 grams) Big Bad Beef Rib Rub (page 45)

1/2 cup (120 milliliters) water

1/2 cup (120 milliliters) oil

1/2 cup (120 grams) Lone Star Beef Sauce (page 48)

Get your fire going, with your grill set up for indirect smoking as described in chapter 1.

While that's happening, remove the membrane from the back of your beef ribs. Sprinkle all but 2 tablespoons of the rub evenly over the ribs. Mix the remaining rub with the water and oil, to make a mop.

Fire's ready! Throw your beef ribs on the grill, and smoke them for at least 2 hours, and 3 won't hurt a bit. After the first 30 minutes, mop them with the oil/water/rub mixture every time you add chips or chunks to the grill.

When the meat is tender and starting to shrink back from the bones, serve with the Lone Star Beef Sauce.

YIELD: 4–5 servings

Assuming 5 servings, each serving will have 8 grams of carbohydrate and 2 grams of fiber, for a usable carb count of 6 grams, not including the polyols in the rub and the sauce; 46 grams protein.

⁂ Five-Spice Beef Ribs

You can add a finishing sauce to these if you like—the Five-Spice Barbecue Sauce would be the obvious choice—but these are truly awesome with no finishing sauce at all. Furthermore, serving them with no finishing sauce makes them very low carb.

> 1 rack beef ribs, 2 1/2–3 pounds (1.5 kilograms)
> 1 batch Five-Spice Beef Rub (page 49)
> 1 batch Five-Spice Beef Mop (page 50)

First, get your fire going, with your grill set up for indirect smoking as described in chapter 1.

Next, remove the membrane from the back of your beef ribs. Sprinkle the ribs all over with the Five-Spice Beef Rub. (You'll have used 1 1/2 teaspoons of the rub in the mop; feel free to use all the rest on your ribs.) When your fire is ready, put your ribs on the grill, add the chips or chunks, close the lid, and let them smoke for a half hour. Then start mopping every 30–45 minutes, whenever you add more chips or chunks. Let your ribs smoke 2–3 hours, or until the meat is shrinking back from the bone.

That's it! These truly don't need another thing.

YIELD: 4–5 servings

Assuming 5 servings, each will have 2 grams of carbohydrate and 1 gram of fiber, for a usable carb count of 1 gram; 45 grams protein.

☀ Peppery Smoked Lamb

This is really wonderful. If you're serving a crowd, feel free to double the rub and the mop and do a whole leg.

> 3–4-pound (2-kilogram) section of a leg of lamb
> Peppery Lamb Rub (page 71)
> Lamb Mop (page 72)

The whole thing is pretty simple; it just takes some time. Place your lamb on a platter and sprinkle it liberally all over with the Peppery Lamb Rub. Let it sit for at least a half hour, and more won't hurt a bit (but if you're letting it sit for a while, you'll want to refrigerate it, of course).

Start your grill, and set it up for indirect cooking. Put a drip pan under the unlit side of the grill, and place the lamb over it. Add soaked wood chips or chunks, and close the grill. Smoke your lamb, following the instructions in chapter 1, for about 2 hours or until a meat thermometer registers 160°F–170°F (75°C–80°C). Let the lamb sit for 20 minutes before carving.

YIELD: How many servings you get will depend on the size of your piece of lamb. Figure roughly 2 servings per pound.

It's impossible to know exactly how many grams of carbohydrate you'll get from the rub and the mop, but it's very unlikely to be any more than 2–3 grams. About 32 grams of protein per serving.

Burgers

Okay, so you'll probably just have regular old burgers at some of your cook-outs, but if you get tired of plain burgers with no bun, try one of these!

☀ Chipotle Cheeseburgers

These are truly great; my husband and I couldn't stop talking about how well this recipe worked out! Of course, since I have to keep cooking new stuff, we won't get to eat these again till 2012. But still, just amazing.

    2 pounds (1 kilogram) ground beef
    6 chipotle chiles canned in adobo sauce, minced
    1/2 cup (30 grams) chopped cilantro
    2 cloves garlic, crushed
    1/4 cup (40 grams) minced onion
    1/2 teaspoon salt
    6 ounces (170 grams) Monterey Jack cheese, sliced

Plunk everything but the cheese into a big bowl, and using clean hands, mush everything together until very well blended. Form into 6 burgers about 1" (2.5 centimeters) thick. Put your burgers on a plate and stick 'em in the fridge to chill for a good hour—it makes them easier to handle on the grill.

Get your fire going—you'll want your gas grill on medium or a little lower, or well-ashed charcoal. Grill your burgers for a good 7–10 minutes per side, or until juices run clear, keeping down flare-ups with a water bottle. When burgers are almost done, top with the cheese and let it melt. Serve with Chipotle Sauce (page 58).

YIELD: 6 servings

Exclusive of Chipotle Sauce, each serving will have 1 gram of carbohydrate and 1 gram of fiber, for a usable carb count of 0 grams; 33 grams protein.

☀ Paprika Burgers

Looking for something new to do with the eternal hamburger, I thought of the middle European flavors of Stroganoff and paprikash, and invented this burger.

   2 pounds (1 kilogram) ground beef

   1/2 cup (80 grams) minced onion

   2 tablespoons paprika

   2 tablespoons tomato paste

   2 tablespoons Worcestershire sauce

   2 teaspoons salt

   Sour cream or plain yogurt (optional)

Throw everything in a bowl, and using clean hands, smoosh it all together until well blended. Form into 6 burgers, and put 'em on a plate. Stash 'em in the fridge to chill for an hour.

Okay, light your grill—set your gas grill to medium or a little lower, or wait until your charcoal has burned down to well-ashed coals. Throw your burgers on the grill, and cook for 7–10 minutes per side, keeping down flare-ups with your water bottle. Serve these with a dollop of sour cream or plain yogurt on top, if you like, to keep the Mitteleuropa theme going.

YIELD: 6 servings

Exclusive of sour cream or yogurt, each will have 4 grams of carbohydrate and 1 gram of fiber, for a usable carb count of 3 grams; 28 grams protein; 489 calories. 1 tablespoon sour cream will add 1 gram of carbohydrate, 0 grams fiber, a trace of protein, and 31 calories. 1 tablespoon of plain yogurt will add 1 gram of carbohydrate (less, if you go by the GO-Diet's count of 4 grams of carbohydrate per cup), 0 grams fiber, and 1 gram protein.

☀ Jamie's Elvis Burgers

Credit where credit is due: this recipe was inspired by one demonstrated by Jamie Oliver on his Food Network show *Oliver's Twist*—he made some burgers for an Elvis impersonator friend. They looked very tasty but had too much onion and a pile of bread crumbs in them, and, of course, Jamie served his on a bun. Plus he's a serious purist who grinds his own beef, not to mention his own spices. This version is both easier and considerably lower in carbs—but still unusually tasty.

> 2 pounds (1 kilogram) ground chuck
>
> 2/3 cup (100 grams) minced red onion
>
> 1 tablespoon olive oil
>
> 1/2 teaspoon ground cumin
>
> 1 tablespoon ground coriander
>
> 1 pinch salt
>
> 1 teaspoon ground pepper
>
> 2 tablespoons Parmesan cheese
>
> 1 1/2 tablespoons spicy mustard

Just plop everything into a large mixing bowl, and mush it all together with clean hands until it's well combined. Form into 6 burgers, about 1" (2.5 centimeters) thick. Put 'em on a plate and chill for at least an hour before grilling.

Get your fire going—you'll want your gas grill on medium or a little lower, or well-ashed charcoal. Grill for 7–10 minutes per side, keeping flare-ups down with a squirt bottle of water, until juices run clear. Serve with Dana's No-Sugar Ketchup (page 30) and some dill pickles, if you like.

YIELD: 6 servings

Each serving will have 3 grams of carbohydrate, a trace of fiber, and 28 grams of protein.

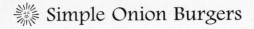 Simple Onion Burgers

- 2 pounds (1 kilogram) ground beef
- 3 tablespoons onion soup mix
- 2 teaspoons hot sauce
- 2 teaspoons Worcestershire sauce
- ¼ teaspoon pepper

Just plop everything in a big mixing bowl, and use clean hands to smoosh it together. Form into 6 patties, put 'em on a plate, and chill 'em for an hour or so before grilling them over a medium gas grill, or well-ashed charcoal. As always, have your water bottle on hand for keeping down flare-ups, and give the burgers about 7–10 minutes per side.

YIELD: 6 servings

Each serving will have 4 grams of carbohydrate and 1 gram of fiber, for a usable carb count of 3 grams; 26 grams protein.

☀ Kofta Burgers

Kofta kebabs are kebabs of curried ground lamb, formed around skewers. Seemed to me that it would be easier just to make my seasoned lamb into burgers, so that's what I did.

2 pounds (1 kilogram) ground lamb

1 cup (160 grams) minced onion

2 tablespoons curry powder

¼ cup (60 grams) plain yogurt

2 cloves garlic, crushed

Just plop everything into a mixing bowl—do make sure your onion is pretty finely minced or your burgers will want to crumble on you—and, using clean hands, smoosh it all together until it's well blended. Form into 6 burgers about 1" (2.5 centimeters) thick. Chill them for an hour before grilling; then grill over a medium fire for 7–10 minutes per side. Serve with Cucumber-Yogurt Sauce (page 136).

YIELD: 6 servings

Exclusive of the sauce, each will have 4 grams of carbohydrate and 1 gram of fiber, for a usable carb count of 3 grams; 26 grams protein.

☀ Cucumber-Yogurt Sauce

   1/2 cup (60 grams) shredded cucumber

   1 cup (230 grams) plain yogurt

   1 clove garlic, crushed

   1/4 teaspoon salt

   1 pinch ground cumin

   1 pinch coriander

   4 tablespoons chopped cilantro

Plunk the shredded cucumber into a strainer over a bowl or in the sink. You want to let some moisture drain out of it.

Open your yogurt and pour off any whey that's gathered. (The whey is the clear liquid that sometimes gathers around yogurt.) Dump your yogurt into a bowl, and add the garlic, salt, cumin, and coriander. Now go back to your cucumber, and press it with clean hands or the back of a spoon to get most of the water out. Add your drained cucumber into the bowl with the yogurt, and stir everything up. Add the cilantro, stir again, and serve with Kofta Burgers (page 135) or anything curried.

YIELD: 6 servings

Each serving will have 3 grams of carb—actually closer to 2, if you use the GO-Diet's figure of 4 grams per cup of plain yogurt—a trace of fiber, and 2 grams of protein.

About Chuck Steak

A lot of people think beef chuck is good only for pot roasting or other moist cooking techniques because it's not as tender as some other cuts are. But it's important to remember the basic rule of thumb where meat is involved: the more tender the meat, the less flavorful it is. That's because tender cuts come from muscles the animal didn't use much, while tougher cuts come from muscles the animal used more, creating more connective tissue—and more taste!

Fortunately, if you treat chuck to some tenderizer and a good marinade, it can be grilled and still come out just as tender as you please—while offering a robust flavor not often found in a sirloin or other pricier cuts. Don't worry about the meat tenderizer, by the way—it's actually a naturally occurring papaya enzyme and completely harmless. You can use any brand of tenderizer you like, but I favor a brand called Indo, made by Modern Products (the same people who make my beloved Vege-Sal) and found at many health food stores.

☀ Chuckwagon Steak

2–2 1/2 pounds (1 kilogram) boneless beef chuck steak, 1 1/2–2"
(4 centimeters) thick

2 teaspoons meat tenderizer

1 cup (225 milliliters) olive oil

1/4 cup (60 milliliters) cider vinegar

2/3 cup (160 milliliters) lime juice

Sprinkle half the tenderizer evenly over one side of the chuck, and pierce the meat all over with a fork. Turn it over and repeat on the other side, using the other teaspoon of tenderizer.

Now, put the meat in a flat, shallow, nonreactive pan that fits it fairly closely, or in a big zipper-lock bag. Mix together the rest of the ingredients and pour them over the steak. If you're using a bag, press out the air, seal it up, and turn it a few times to coat the whole piece of meat. If you're using a pan, turn the meat over once, again, to coat it. Stick the whole thing in the fridge, and let your meat marinate for at least several hours, turning it a few times.

When dinnertime rolls around (or actually a bit beforehand), get your grill going—you'll want your charcoal to be white, or your gas grill on medium or a touch higher. Just pull your steak out and grill it—about 12 minutes per side puts it at about the degree of doneness I like, but cook it to your liking; then slice it across the grain.

This is great plain, but it's also a good choice to serve with the Cilantro Chimichurri (page 59).

YIELD: 6 servings

If you drank the marinade, each serving would have 3 grams of carbohydrate and a trace of fiber, but, of course, you drain the marinade off. I'd count no more than 1 gram of carbohydrate per serving, and I suspect that's a generous estimate; 30 grams of protein.

☀ Uptown Chuck

2 teaspoons meat tenderizer

2–2 1/2 pounds (1 kilogram) boneless chuck steak, 1 1/2–2" (4 centimeters) thick

1/2 cup (120 milliliters) canola oil

1/4 cup (60 milliliters) soy sauce

1/2 cup (120 milliliters) dry red wine

1 tablespoon grated gingerroot

2 teaspoons curry powder

2 tablespoons Dana's No-Sugar Ketchup (page 30)

1/4 teaspoon pepper

1 teaspoon Tabasco sauce

The drill is pretty much the same as in the previous recipe: sprinkle half the tenderizer over one side of the steak, pierce it all over with a fork, turn it, and repeat with the rest of the tenderizer. This one works best with a shallow, flat, nonreactive pan—place the steak in it, mix everything else together and pour it over the steak; then turn the steak over to coat both sides with the marinade. Stick the whole thing in the fridge, and let it marinate, turning it over when you think of it, for at least several hours, and overnight is even better.

Once you have your grill going and your coals are white, or your gas grill is heated, grill your steak for about 12 minutes per side, or to your liking, basting a few times with the marinade (but quitting with at least five minutes to spare, so the germs get killed). Slice across the grain, and serve.

YIELD: 6 servings

3 grams of carbohydrate per serving, but again, that assumes you consume all of the marinade. I'd count no more than 1 gram per serving; 25 grams of protein.

☀ Carne Asada Steak

Carne asada is Spanish for "grilled beef"—well, actually, "meat," but beef is assumed. It's a Mexican and Southwestern specialty. I don't know how authentic my version is, but it sure tastes good, especially with an ice-cold light beer.

2 pounds (1 kilogram) boneless round steak, or chuck, 1 1/2–2"
   (4 centimeters) thick

2 teaspoons meat tenderizer

1/2 cup (120 milliliters) red wine vinegar

1/4 cup (60 milliliters) olive oil

2 tablespoons Dana's No-Sugar Ketchup (page 30)

1 tablespoon soy sauce

2 cloves garlic, crushed

2 teaspoons ground or rubbed sage

1/2 teaspoon salt

1 teaspoon dry mustard

1 teaspoon paprika

2 jalapenos, minced

Sprinkle one side of your meat with 1 teaspoon of the tenderizer, and pierce it all over with a fork. Turn it over, and treat the other side the same way with the second teaspoon of tenderizer.

Put your meat in a large zipper-lock bag or in a shallow, nonreactive pan. Mix together everything else (wash your hands after handling those jalapenos!) and pour it over the meat. If you're using a bag, press out the air, seal it, and turn it a few times to coat the meat; if you're using a pan, turn the meat over once or twice to coat. Put the meat in the refrigerator and let it marinate for at least several hours—overnight is better—turning it now and then.

When dinnertime rolls around, let your charcoal burn down to the well-ashed stage, or set your gas grill to medium, and grill your steak for about 10 minutes per side, basting frequently with the marinade. Stop basting 5 minutes or so before you're done grilling, to make sure the germs get killed. If you'd like, you can put the leftover marinade in a microwavable bowl or in a saucepan and either microwave it until it's boiled for a minute or bring it to a boil on the stove, then serve it as a sauce.

YIELD: 6 servings

If you do use the leftover marinade as a sauce, and eat all of it, each serving will have 3 grams of carbohydrate, and a trace of fiber, for a usable carb count of 3 grams; 29 grams of protein.

☀ Ginger Marinated Chuck

I have a yummy pot roast recipe that calls for tomatoes, cider vinegar, and ginger, so this idea was a natural.

2 pounds (1 kilogram) boneless chuck, 1 1/2–2" (4 centimeters) thick

2 teaspoons meat tenderizer

1/4 cup (60 grams) Dana's No-Sugar Ketchup (page 30)

1/4 cup (60 milliliters) Paul Newman vinaigrette

2 1/2 tablespoons Splenda

1/2 teaspoon blackstrap molasses

2 teaspoons grated gingerroot

1/2 teaspoon salt

1 tablespoon water

1 tablespoon cider vinegar

1/2 teaspoon soy sauce

First, do your thing with the tenderizer—sprinkle a teaspoon of it over one side of the meat, pierce it all over with a fork, flip it over, and repeat with the rest of the tenderizer. Now put your meat in a large zipper-lock bag or in a shallow, nonreactive pan, mix together everything else, and pour it over the meat. If you're using a zipper-lock bag, press out the air and seal it. Either way, turn your chuck steak over once or twice, to make sure it's coated with the marinade. Stash it in the fridge, and let it marinate for at least several hours, and overnight is better.

When it's time to cook, get the grill going, setting your gas grill to medium or letting your charcoal get a good coat of ash. Pull your steak out of the marinade and grill it for about 10 minutes per side, basting frequently with the marinade. Stop basting with five minutes to spare, so any germs get killed!

YIELD: 6 servings

Each serving will have 3 grams of carbohydrate—again, if you consume all of the marinade. I'd count no more than 1 gram of carbohydrate per serving, and 24 grams of protein.

Cape Town Lamb Steaks

You can use lamb chops instead, but I like steaks cut from a leg of lamb. When I buy a whole leg, I ask the nice meat guy to slice some steaks from the center, leaving me two small roasts from either end. Since leg of lamb is often as cheap as $1.99 a pound around here, while lamb chops are usually over $4.99 a pound, this is also economical!

   2 tablespoons Worcestershire sauce

   2 tablespoons soy sauce

   2 tablespoons Splenda

   1/4 teaspoon blackstrap molasses

   1 tablespoon plus 1 teaspoon dry mustard

   1 tablespoon plus 1 teaspoon lemon juice

   1 tablespoon plus 1 teaspoon olive oil

   2 cloves garlic, crushed

   2 teaspoons grated gingerroot

   1 pound (500 grams) lamb leg steaks, about 1/2" (1.25 centimeters) thick

First get your grill going—set your gas grill to medium to medium-low, or let your coals get thoroughly white.

Mix together everything but the steaks. Brush the steaks liberally with the sauce, then grill for about 7 minutes per side, basting frequently. If you like, bring any left-over sauce to a boil (to kill the raw lamb germs) and serve with the steaks at the table.

YIELD: 2 servings

If you do eat all of the sauce, each serving will have 5 grams of carbohydrate, a trace of fiber, and 33 grams of protein.

chapter six

Fish and Seafood

Tired of all that slow smoke cooking, or just don't have the time? Fish grills up quickly and with great results. You know how healthy fish is, of course, and if you're counting calories as well as carbohydrates, fish has far lower calories than most of the other cookout choices. But if you want to have a sort of upscale cookout, fish or seafood also somehow seems more, well, elegant than burgers, ribs, or chicken. Even good old catfish takes on a new flair!

Just remember, fish is delicate, so oil your grill well or spray it with non-stick cooking spray (take it off of the fire first—that stuff is very flammable!). And don't overcook it!

Okay, somebody cue Paul Hogan: "Throw another shrimp on the barbie!"

☀ Wasabi Soy Salmon

Wasabi is sometimes called Japanese horseradish. I don't know about that; to me, wasabi tastes like wasabi, but it does have that hot-and-pungent sinus-clearing quality! That pungency makes the Wasabi Baste a great foil for the richness of salmon.

>   1 whole salmon, cleaned and head removed, between 6 and 7 pounds
>   (3 kilograms)
>   1 batch Wasabi Baste (page 61)

Get your grill going first. If you're using charcoal, once the coals are ash covered you'll want to use fireproof tongs to arrange them in a strip roughly the length and width of your fish. Either way, charcoal or gas, you'll want a medium-hot fire.

While the fire's readying itself, make several slashes on either side of your salmon, down to the bone. This will help it cook through before you char the outside. Now, baste the fish all over, including inside the body cavity and into the slashes, with the Wasabi Baste. Set your fish over the fire, on a well-oiled grill. Close the lid, and set a timer for 10 minutes. When the timer goes off, baste the "up" side of your fish and inside the body cavity again. Re-close the grill hood and cook for another 10 minutes or so.

Now, using two metal spatulas, carefully roll your fish over, and re-situate it over the fire. Baste the "up" side and the body cavity, and close the lid again. Set the timer for 10 minutes again, and baste once more when it goes off. Close the lid, and grill for a final 10 minutes. At this point your salmon should flake easily, and an instant-read thermometer stuck in the thickest part should read between 135°F and 140°F (60°C).

Very carefully lift your salmon off the grill with your two spatulas, place on a platter, and serve.

YIELD: A 6 ½-pound salmon will serve at least 12 people!

Each serving will have no more than 1 gram of carbohydrate, and will have 49 grams of protein—plus lots of heart-healthy fish oil!

☀ Lemon-Herb Stuffed Salmon

This is a great recipe to serve at a party, since it will feed a dozen or more people. It will impress them, too!

> 1 whole salmon, cleaned and head removed, between 6 and 7 pounds
>   (3 kilograms)
> 1 lemon, sliced as thinly as humanly possible
> 6 scallions, any wilted bits trimmed, and sliced very thinly lengthways
> 4 tablespoons fresh oregano leaves, minced
> 1 tablespoon fresh thyme leaves, stripped off their stems

First, get your fire going. If you're using charcoal, once the coals are ash covered you'll want to use fireproof tongs to arrange them in a strip roughly the length and width of your fish. Either way, charcoal or gas, you'll want a medium-hot fire.

Lay your salmon out on a platter. Stuff the lemon slices into the body cavity, distributing them evenly along the length of the fish. Do the same with the scallions. Mix together the two herbs, and stuff them into the body cavity as well.

Now, run toothpicks or skewers through the edges of the fish and use twine to lace around the skewers to hold the edge of the fish closed. Or, if you prefer, use a big needle and heavy thread to sew your salmon closed.

Slash the fish every couple of inches, down to the bone, to let the heat in. Now place the fish on an oiled grill over the fire, and close the lid. After 15–20 minutes, turn the salmon very carefully, using two spatulas, and re-situate it over the fire. Re-close the lid, and give your salmon another 15–20 minutes. It's done when it flakes easily and an instant-read thermometer registers between 135°F and 140°F (60°C). Use your two spatulas to carefully remove your fish to a platter, and serve.

YIELD: 12 servings

Each serving will have just 1 gram of carbohydrate, a trace of fiber, and 49 grams of protein.

 # Chipotle Garlic Salmon

1 batch Chipotle Garlic Butter (page 57)

2 pounds (1 kilogram) salmon fillets, cut in serving-sized pieces

Start your grill heating; you'll want medium-high heat.

Next, put your Chipotle Garlic Butter in a small saucepan, and place it over lowest heat—you want to melt it so you can brush it on your fish. While it's melting, cut your fish into servings, and lay it out on a platter.

When the Chipotle Garlic Butter is melted, brush the fish fillets all over with it. Then lay the fish on an oiled grill. Because the buttery baste can cause flare-ups, you'll want to have a squirt bottle of water on hand, and keep a close watch.

Grill the fish about 5 minutes per side, or until flaky clear through. Baste frequently while cooking, quitting a few minutes before the fish is done, to make sure that all the germs are killed. Serve.

YIELD: 6 servings

Each serving will have only a trace of carbohydrate, and 31 grams of protein.

☀ Maple-Balsamic Glazed Salmon

This was amazingly popular with friends when I served it at a dinner party. Feel free to double this!

   2 tablespoons extra-virgin olive oil

   1/4 cup (60 milliliters) sugar-free pancake syrup

   2 cloves garlic, crushed

   1/2 teaspoon salt

   2 tablespoons balsamic vinegar

   1 pound (500 grams) salmon fillet

 Mix together everything but the salmon, and set aside half the mixture. Cut the salmon into 3 or 4 serving pieces (if you didn't buy it in serving-sized pieces), lay them on a plate, and brush both sides of each piece of salmon with half of the pancake-syrup mixture. Grill the salmon over well-ashed coals, or over a gas grill set to medium-low, about 5 minutes per side or until done through. Place on serving plates, drizzle with reserved baste, and serve.

YIELD: 4 servings

Each serving will have 1 gram of carbohydrate, not including the polyols in the sugar-free pancake syrup; a trace of fiber; and 23 grams protein.

☀ Citrus Catfish

Squeezing a little lemon over fish is a culinary classic—but this goes way beyond just lemon!

1 1/2 pounds (700 grams) catfish fillets

1/2 cup (120 milliliters) lemon juice

1/2 teaspoon orange extract

4 tablespoons soy sauce

2 tablespoons plus 2 teaspoons Splenda

2 cloves garlic, crushed

1/4 teaspoon pepper

Lay the fillets on a plate with a rim—a pie plate (or two) is ideal. Combine everything else and pour it over the fillets, turning to coat both sides. Let the fillets marinate for at least 15 minutes, a half hour won't hurt. Heat the grill, or get a fire going, in the meanwhile.

Make sure your grill is well oiled, and grill your catfish over medium heat or well-ashed coals, for about 5 minutes per side, basting it on both sides with the marinade when you turn it—which you'll want to do carefully! When the fish is opaque and flaky, it's ready to serve.

YIELD: 3 servings

6 grams of carb if you eat all of the marinade—I'd put it closer to 4 grams, a trace of fiber, and 29 grams of protein.

 Indonesian Grilled Catfish

Low carb, low fat, low cal—this recipe is low in everything but flavor!

  4 catfish fillets

  1/4 cup (60 milliliters) soy sauce

  1 tablespoon rice wine vinegar

  1 teaspoon Splenda

  1 drop blackstrap molasses (if you keep your blackstrap in a squeeze bottle,
      it's easy to measure just 1 drop)

  1 teaspoon grated gingerroot

  1 clove garlic, crushed

Lay your catfish in a glass pie plate. Mix together everything else and pour over the catfish, turning to coat. Stash the whole thing in the fridge for at least a half hour, and a few hours would be great. Flip the fish over halfway through if you think of it, to marinate both sides evenly.

When marinating time is up, pull the fish out and throw it on a well-oiled grill over a medium fire. It shouldn't take more than 3–5 minutes per side to be flaky and done—turn it carefully!

This is good served with a cucumber salad.

YIELD: 4 servings

Each serving will have 2 grams of carbohydrate, a trace of fiber, and 27 grams of protein.

☀ Tuna Steaks with Peach-Citrus Relish

The quantity of relish is small here, to keep the carb count low—just enough to point up the flavor of the fish.

> 1 ripe peach
>
> 1 tablespoon lime juice
>
> 1/4 teaspoon orange extract
>
> 1 clove garlic, crushed
>
> 1 tablespoon Splenda
>
> 1/2 tablespoon soy sauce
>
> 2 pounds (1 kilogram) tuna steaks
>
> Olive oil

First peel your peach, cut it in half, remove the stone, and dice it small. Stir in the lime juice, orange extract, garlic, Splenda, and soy sauce. Set this aside—indeed, you can do this a few hours in advance if you like, and refrigerate the relish until dinnertime. If you do this, get your relish out of the fridge before you get ready to grill the fish—it will have more flavor at room temperature.

When it's time to cook, either light a charcoal fire and let the coals burn down till they're ash covered, or set your gas grill to medium. Cut your tuna steaks into serving portions and rub each one lightly with olive oil. Make sure your grill is well oiled, then grill the tuna no more than 3–5 minutes per side—it should still be red in the middle. (I learned this the hard way. Cook a tuna steak until it's pink clear through, and it will be dry and tough.) Divide the relish between the portions, and serve.

YIELD: 4 servings

Each serving will have 4 grams of carbohydrate and 1 gram of fiber, for a usable carb count of 3 grams; and 53 grams protein.

☀ Citrus-Ginger Mahi Mahi

2 tablespoons lemon juice

1/4 teaspoon orange extract

2 teaspoons soy sauce

1/2 teaspoon Splenda

1 tablespoon grated gingerroot

1 tablespoon oil

1 pound (500 grams) mahi mahi fillets

This goes fast, so if you're using a charcoal grill, light it before starting to prepare your food so you're not hanging around waiting for your fire to be ready.

On a plate with a rim, or a glass pie plate, mix together everything but the fish. Lay the fish in the marinade and turn it over to coat. Let it sit for 15–30 minutes, at which point you want your grill to be medium-hot. Grill for just 5–6 minutes per side. Baste both sides once with the marinade when you turn it.

YIELD: 2–3 servings

Assuming 2 servings, each will have 2 grams of carbohydrate—actually less, because you won't finish the marinade—a trace of fiber, and 41 grams protein.

☀ Bacon-Wrapped Grilled Trout

This is simple and classic.

> 4 medium rainbow trout, cleaned, heads removed
> 8 sprigs fresh rosemary
> 8 slices bacon

Stuff the rosemary into the body cavities of the trout. Now, wrap each trout with 2 slices of bacon, covering as much of the skin of each fish as you can. Hold in place with toothpicks you've soaked in water for a half hour or so. (It can be tough to get the toothpicks through the fish skin—use a metal skewer, a nut pick, or the point of a knife to assist, if needed.)

Grill over a medium fire, keeping down flare-ups with your water bottle, until the bacon is done, and serve.

YIELD: 4 servings

Each serving will have 1 gram of carbohydrate and a trace of fiber (which you'll get only if you eat the rosemary), and about 45 grams protein.

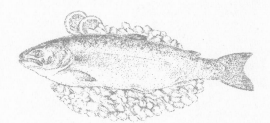

☀ Brined, Jerked Red Snapper

Had one too many meals of dried-out fish? Try brining it!

  2 pounds (1 kilogram) red snapper fillets

  Brine:
  1/3 cup (100 grams) kosher salt
  3 quarts (3 liters) water
  2 tablespoons jerk rub (either homemade or purchased)

  Seasonings:
  4 cloves garlic, crushed
  8 teaspoons olive oil
  1 rounded tablespoon jerk rub (purchased, or from the recipe on page 63)
  1/4 cup (60 milliliters) lemon juice
  4 teaspoons soy sauce
  4 scallions, sliced

In a shallow, nonreactive container big enough to hold your fish fillets, dissolve the salt in the water—this is easier if the water's warm. Stir in the jerk rub. If you've used warm water, let it cool to no more than tepid before adding your fish fillets. Make sure they're submerged in the brine, and let them sit for 1–2 hours.

Okay, time's up. Get your fire going now, if you're using charcoal, so it will be ready when you are. Drain the brine off of your fish. In a rimmed plate or pie plate, mix together the garlic and olive oil, then stir in the jerk rub, lemon juice, and soy sauce. Lay your brined fillets in this marinade, turning them over once or twice to coat. Let the fillets sit for 15 minutes or so. Then grill over a medium fire, 3-5 minutes per side. Baste both sides with the seasoning mixture when you turn the fish—but not after that.

When the fish is flaky, remove to serving plates, and top each fillet with a sliced scallion.

YIELD: 4 servings

Each serving will have 4 grams of carbohydrate and 1 gram of fiber, for a usable carb count of 3 grams (less if you make your own sugar-free jerk rub); 41 grams protein.

☀ Brined Shrimp

Brining shrimp makes them plumper and firmer—some say the texture resembles lobster. Adds flavor, too! I mean, what is sea water but a kind of brine? If you want to be terribly authentic, use sea salt!

    2 tablespoons kosher salt or large-crystal sea salt
    1 quart (1 liter) cold water
    2 tablespoons Splenda
    1/4 teaspoon blackstrap molasses
    1 pound (500 grams) shrimp in the shell—whatever size you like

Dissolve the salt in the water. Stir in the Splenda and molasses. Now pour this mixture over your shrimp, in a bowl or in a large zipper-lock bag. If you're using a bag, press out the air and seal it. Either way, make sure your shrimp are submerged. Let them sit in the brine for 30–45 minutes for medium-sized shrimp, or as much as an hour for really huge ones.

Now your shrimp are ready to cook! See the following pages for two simple things to do with them.

Brined Lemon Pepper Shrimp

1 pound (500 grams) brined, uncooked shrimp in the shell

2 cloves garlic

¼ cup (60 milliliters) olive oil

2 tablespoons lemon pepper

While your shrimp are brining, crush the garlic and pour the olive oil over it. That way, you'll have garlic-flavored olive oil by the time the shrimp are ready to cook.

Drain the brine off of the shrimp and pat them dry with a paper towel. Put the shrimp in a bowl, pour the garlic olive oil over them, and toss. Now sprinkle the lemon pepper over them, and toss again.

You'll need a small-holed grill rack or a grill wok—I like to use a grill wok for this. Lift your shrimp out of the olive oil with a fork, to let the excess oil drip off, and put over a medium-hot fire. Grill quickly, turning two or three times, until pink clear through—the timing will depend on the size of your shrimp, but it shouldn't take more than 6 or 7 minutes. If the olive oil causes flare-ups, keep them down with your squirt bottle.

YIELD: 3–4 servings

Assuming 3, each serving would have 6 grams of carb—if you drank the brine (but you won't, of course). So figure no more than 4 grams per serving, a trace of fiber, and 31 grams of protein. (You'll actually get a little more protein if you cook big shrimp than if you cook little ones, because of the better shrimp-to-shell ratio.).

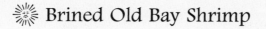 Brined Old Bay Shrimp

   1 pound (500 grams) brined, uncooked shrimp in the shell

   ¼ cup (60 milliliters) olive oil

   2 tablespoons Old Bay Seasoning (look for this in the spice aisle)

This is, er, remarkably similar to the previous recipe. Drain your brined shrimp and pat them dry. Put 'em in a bowl, pour the olive oil over them, and toss. Sprinkle the Old Bay Seasoning over the shrimp, and toss again. Grill on a small-holed grill rack or in a grill wok, over a medium-hot fire, until pink clear through—no more than 7 minutes or so—then serve.

YIELD: 3–4 servings

Assuming 3, this would have 3 grams of carbohydrate per serving—again, if you drank the brine. So figure about 2 grams per serving, with no fiber, and 31 grams of protein.

chapter seven

Kebabs

As cooking things over an outdoor fire goes, kebabs are the polar opposite of true barbecue: Instead of cooking large-ish hunks of food slowly for very long periods of time, we cut up things into little bitty pieces (or use things that naturally come in little bitty pieces, like shrimp and scallops) and cook them quickly. To keep them from falling through the grill, and to make them easy to handle, we thread the little bitty pieces of food on skewers. That threading bits of food on skewers makes them seem more, well, spiffy somehow, is just a bonus!

Another benefit is that cutting up things into little bitty pieces gives them lots of surface area, so marinades and bastes can be absorbed more readily, making for great flavor and letting us tenderize meat, if need be, by using acidic ingredients like vinegar or lemon juice.

You'll notice that these recipes all tell you to soak bamboo skewers in water for at least 30 minutes before threading things onto them. This is because if you use bamboo skewers without soaking them in water, they'll catch fire. However, if you have metal skewers, feel free to use them instead—but be aware that your kebabs may cook a little quicker on metal skewers because they conduct heat.

⁎ Balsamic-Olive Beef Kebabs

A rich, full flavor.

> 1 pound (500 grams) beef round roast, trimmed
>
> 1/2 cup (120 milliliters) olive oil
>
> 1/4 cup (60 milliliters) balsamic vinegar
>
> 1 clove garlic, crushed
>
> About 16 stuffed green olives
>
> 1/2 medium onion
>
> Salt and pepper

Cut your beef into cubes about 1 1/2 inches (4 cm) square. Put them in a nonreactive bowl or in a large zipper-lock bag. Combine the olive oil, balsamic vinegar, and garlic, and pour over the beef cubes. If you're using a bowl, stir the whole thing up to coat the cubes. If you're using a zipper-lock bag, press out the air, seal it, and turn it a few times to coat. Either way, throw your cubes in the fridge and let them marinate for at least a few hours. If you're going to use bamboo skewers, this is a good time to put them in water to soak, too.

When it's time to cook, first get your fire going. You'll want to set a gas grill on medium, or let coals get well covered with ash.

Now, pull out your beef cubes, not to mention your olives and an onion. Cut the onion in half, and put one half back in the fridge for another day. Cut the other half into quarters. Separate the onion into its separate layers. Drain the marinade off of your beef cubes, reserving it for basting.

Skewer a beef cube, then an olive, then a layer of onion, then a beef cube, and so forth. Build all three skewers evenly. Salt and pepper the kebabs lightly.

Fire ready? Throw your kebabs on the grill and cook for about 7–10 minutes per side, basting a few times with the reserved marinade. You want them done through but still a little pink in the center.

YIELD: 3 servings

Each serving will have 5 grams of carbohydrate and 1 gram of fiber, for a usable carb count of 4 grams; 34 grams of protein.

☀ Middle Eastern Shish Kebabs

Serve this with the Cucumber-Tomato Salad (page 212) for a Middle Eastern feast.

1 1/2 pounds (700 grams) boneless lamb (leg or shoulder)

1/2 cup (120 milliliters) olive oil

1/2 cup (120 milliliters) red wine vinegar

1 clove garlic, crushed

1 teaspoon ground cumin

1 medium onion

Salt and pepper

Cut the lamb into cubes about 1 1/2" (4 centimeters) square. Put them in a nonreactive bowl or in a large zipper-lock bag. Mix together the olive oil, vinegar, garlic, and cumin, and pour over the lamb cubes. If using a bowl, stir to make sure cubes are coated. If using a bag, press out the air, seal the bag, and turn it a few times to coat. Either way, let your lamb marinate for at least several hours. If you're going to use bamboo skewers, this is a good time to put them in water to soak. You'll need 4 skewers.

Okay, dinnertime has rolled around. Get your fire going—you'll want to set a gas grill at medium-low or let charcoal cook down pretty well. While that's happening, let's make kebabs.

Peel your onion and cut it into quarters, then into eighths, and separate it into the individual layers. Drain your lamb cubes, saving the marinade. Skewer a lamb cube, then a layer of onion, then another lamb cube, and so forth, filling all four skewers evenly. Salt and pepper your kebabs and throw them on the fire. Grill your skewers slowly, turning often and basting with the reserved marinade, until the meat is well done and tender—at least 20 minutes. Stop basting at least 5 minutes before pulling your skewers off the fire.

YIELD: 4 servings

If you consume all the marinade, each serving will have 5 grams of carbohydrate and 1 gram of fiber. Since you don't, I'd count 3 grams per kebab, and 35 grams of protein.

☀ Caribbean Shrimp Kebabs

The pink shrimp and shredded coconut give this such a festive look!

- ¹/₂ cup (120 grams) crushed canned pineapple in juice
- ¹/₄ cup (60 milliliters) white wine vinegar
- ¹/₄ cup (60 milliliters) Splenda
- ¹/₂ teaspoon blackstrap molasses
- 24 large shrimp, peeled and deveined
- ¹/₄ cup (20 grams) shredded unsweetened coconut (find this at health food stores)

Put the pineapple, vinegar, Splenda, and blackstrap in the blender, and whir them up for a minute. In a nonreactive bowl or zipper-lock bag, pour this mixture over the shrimp. Let them marinate for at least 15 minutes, but not more than an hour. If you're using bamboo skewers, put them in water to soak now, too—you'll need 4 skewers.

While your shrimp are marinating, put your coconut in a small, heavy, dry skillet over a medium flame, and stir it until it just starts to turn golden. Remove from the heat, and reserve.

Get your fire going; you'll want it medium-high. Now skewer your shrimp across their curve—through both the head and tail on each one, so it looks like a cents symbol. You'll have 6 shrimp on each skewer. Make sure your grill is well oiled, and throw your skewers on the fire. They'll need only 3–5 minutes on each side—you'll want to cook them until the shrimp are pink through, but no longer.

If you like, you can boil the pineapple marinade hard for a minute or two, and serve it over the kebabs—this is very, very tasty but does add a few carbs. Either way, sprinkle a tablespoon of the toasted coconut over each skewer before serving.

YIELD: 4 servings

If you eat all of the marinade (yum!), each serving will have 9 grams of carbohydrate and 1 gram of fiber, for a usable carb count of 8 grams; 9 grams protein. If you don't eat the marinade, you can knock 3 or 4 grams of carbohydrate off of that figure.

☀ Thai Basil Shrimp

Shrimp with a sauce that might be called "essence of green." This makes a very classy starter.

> 3/4 cup (30 grams) fresh basil leaves
>
> 3/4 cup (180 milliliters) olive oil
>
> 1 jalapeno (if you can get the little red Thai chilies, use 1 or 2 of those, instead)
>
> 2 teaspoons fish sauce (nuac nam or nam pla)
>
> 2 pounds (1 kilogram) large shrimp, shelled and deveined.

Put 4 bamboo skewers in water to soak at least 1/2 hour before dinner.

Get your fire going before you start cooking—you'll need it medium-hot.

Put the basil, olive oil, jalapeno, and fish sauce in your blender (seed the jalapeno first, and wash your hands afterward!). Run the blender until you have a bright green, intensely herbal-smelling slurry. Set aside 1/4 cup of the mixture in a separate bowl.

Skewer your shrimp across their curve, through the head and the tail, so they look like cents signs. Divide the shrimp evenly between the 4 skewers. Baste your shrimp with the basil mixture, and throw them on the grill. Baste them almost constantly with the basil mixture, and grill for about 4–7 minutes per side or until the shrimp are pink all over. Remove to serving plates, spoon 1 tablespoon of the reserved basil mixture over each skewer, and serve.

YIELD: 4 servings

Each serving will have a mere trace of carbohydrate and fiber, and 19 grams of protein.

☀ Tangerine Chicken Skewers

A fabulous hot hors d'oeuvre for your next outdoor party! My friends loved these.

  3 pounds (1.5 kilograms) boneless, skinless chicken breast

  1/4 medium onion, diced

  1 clove garlic, crushed

  1/4 cup (60 milliliters) olive oil

  1/2 cup (120 milliliters) red wine vinegar

  1/2 cup (120 milliliters) white wine vinegar

  1/2 tablespoon chili garlic paste

  2 tablespoons Splenda

  1 tablespoon lemon juice

  1/2 teaspoon sugar-free imitation honey

  1 12-ounce (360-milliliter) can Diet-Rite tangerine soda

  Salt and pepper

Before you start marinating your chicken, start "marinating" your skewers—soak them in water so they won't go up in flames when you cook later on.

Once that's happening, take a sharp knife and slice the chicken breast just as thin as humanly possible, the long way. It's easier to do this if your chicken is half-frozen. The idea is to reduce your chicken breasts to a pile of very thin strips roughly an inch wide and 4–6 inches long. Put these chicken slivers in a nonreactive bowl or dish of some sort. (For this recipe, an open container is easier than a zipper-lock bag.)

Mix together everything else and pour it over the chicken strips. Give the chicken strips a stir, stick 'em in the fridge, and let them sit there for several hours.

When your party's starting, light the grill. You'll want medium heat. While the grill is heating, weave skewers through the chicken strips: pierce a strip near the end, fold it back and pierce it again, et cetera, until the whole strip is accordioned onto the skewer. I like to do two strips per skewer. Bunch the chicken up a bit on the skewer, rather than stretching it out.

When your chicken is on its skewers, throw the skewers on the grill. These cook quickly—7 minutes total cooking time is about right. Baste halfway through with the marinade, but not after that—germs, you know.

YIELD: This was ample for 12 people as a party snack.

Again, you'll discard most of the marinade, so even though the carb count is theoretically 2 grams per serving, assuming 12 people are sharing these, you'll actually get far less. These are almost carb-free and have 25 grams of protein.

☀ Chicken Kebabs

More interesting than plain old grilled chicken breasts!

- 1 whole green pepper
- 4 whole portobello mushrooms (you can substitute 16 smallish button mushrooms, if you prefer)
- 1 pound (500 grams) boneless, skinless chicken breast
- 1/4 cup (60 milliliters) olive oil
- 2 tablespoons red wine vinegar
- 1 tablespoon lemon juice
- 1 1/2 teaspoons Dijon mustard
- 1 clove garlic, crushed

Have 8 wooden or bamboo skewers soaking in water, or use metal ones.

Core and seed the pepper, and cut it into squares—just quarter it, then quarter each quarter. Cut your portobellos into wedges, too. Cut your chicken into cubes. Thread everything on the skewers in an artful manner, dividing things evenly between the 8 skewers. Now, put the filled skewers into a shallow, nonreactive pan, mix everything else together, and pour it over the kebabs. Turn them to coat, and let them marinate for 20–30 minutes, turning now and then. Then grill over a medium-hot fire, basting frequently, for about 5–7 minutes per side, or until a chunk of chicken is white clear through when you cut it open. Serve two skewers per customer.

Feel free to streamline this recipe if you like, by substituting 1/3 cup bottled Dijon vinaigrette dressing for the marinade—just make sure it's the lowest-carb brand you can find.

YIELD: 4 servings

If you drank the marinade, each serving would have 10 grams of carbohydrate and 2 grams of fiber, for a usable carb count of 8 grams. Since you won't consume all the marinade, it's actually about 7 grams of usable carb per serving, with 29 grams of protein.

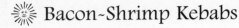# Bacon-Shrimp Kebabs

 2 tablespoons dry white wine

 2 tablespoons oil

 1/2 teaspoon dry mustard

 1 tablespoon chopped fresh parsley

 1 tablespoon dried oregano

 1 tablespoon chopped basil

 2 cloves garlic

 24 medium shrimp, shelled

 6 or 8 slices bacon

Combine the wine, oil, and seasonings in a bowl, and whisk together. Add the shrimp and toss to coat. Let the shrimp marinate for at least 15 minutes, and a half hour won't hurt. Stir them once or twice if you think of it. Meanwhile, soak 3–4 bamboo skewers in water.

 If you're using charcoal, get your grill going before you assemble your kebabs. Skewer a slice of bacon at one end. Next skewer a shrimp—you'll want to go through each shrimp twice, through both the thick end and the thinner end—think of making a cents symbol. Lay the bacon along the shrimp, covering one flat side, and pierce it again. Skewer another shrimp, and run the bacon along the opposite flat side of that shrimp, and pierce the bacon again. (Am I being clear, here? You're covering alternate flat sides of the shrimp with the bacon.) Continue until your skewer has 6 or. 8 shrimp on it, depending on whether you're making 3 or 4 kebabs. You'll need 2 slices of bacon for each skewer. Repeat with your other skewers.

Grill over a medium fire until the bacon is done, basting once or twice with the marinade left in the bowl—but quit basting with a few minutes left to grill, to make sure germs get killed.

YIELD: 3–4 servings

Assuming 3 servings, and assuming you eat every scrap of chopped parsley in the marinade, each serving will have 3 grams of carb and 1 gram of fiber, for a useable carb count of 2 grams; 25 grams of protein.

☀ Lemon-Balsamic Catfish Kebabs

Catfish nuggets are often quite inexpensive, and they're great for making kebabs. Adjust the heat in this recipe by what sort of hot sauce you use— Tabasco if you like it fairly mild, or habañero or Scotch bonnet sauce if you like it spicy!

2 cloves garlic, crushed

2 tablespoons lemon juice

1 tablespoon balsamic vinegar

1 teaspoon soy sauce

1/4 teaspoon ground rosemary

1/4–1/2 teaspoon hot sauce

1 pound (500 grams) catfish nuggets (if your grocery store doesn't
   have catfish nuggets, cut up fillets)

Olive oil

Mix together everything but the catfish and the olive oil in a bowl big enough to hold your catfish nuggets. When the marinade ingredients are blended, add the catfish nuggets and stir them up so they're coated.

Let them marinate for at least 30 minutes—during which time you can be soaking 3 or 4 bamboo skewers in water so they won't catch fire on the grill.

Okay, start your fire; you'll want it at medium or a little lower. Skewer your catfish nuggets, doubling the long ones if necessary to avoid floppy, dangling bits. Pack the nuggets fairly closely to avoid drying. Brush your kebabs with a little olive oil, and make sure your grill is well oiled, too. Now grill your kebabs for about 4–5 minutes per side, or until flaky, then serve.

YIELD: 3–4 kebabs

Assuming 3 servings, each will have 2 grams of carbohydrate (actually less, because you won't eat every drop of the marinade), a trace of fiber, and 25 grams of protein.

☀ Bacon~Wrapped Jerk Scallops

Easy, but impressive! Do use big sea scallops, instead of the smaller bay scallops, for this.

> 32 sea scallops (about a pound)
> Jerk Seasoning (page 63), or use purchased Jerk Seasoning
> 16 slices bacon

Thirty minutes before assembling your kebabs, put 4 bamboo skewers in water to soak.

If your scallops are wet, pat them dry with a paper towel. Put them on a plate and sprinkle them all over with the seasoning. Let them sit while you cut your bacon slices in half, making 32 shorter slices.

Wrap a half slice of bacon around each scallop, going around the circumference. As each one is wrapped, skewer it through where the bacon overlaps and out the other side, to hold. You'll put 8 bacon-wrapped scallops on each skewer. When all your kebabs are assembled, give the exposed flat faces of the scallops another quick sprinkle of seasoning.

Grill, turning once or twice, over a medium-hot fire—have your water bottle on hand for flare-ups. Cook until the bacon is done, and the scallops are fairly firm.

YIELD: 4 servings

Each serving will have about 3 grams of carbohydrate and a trace of fiber, and 21 grams of protein.

☀ Lemon-Maple Scallop Kebabs

These are bacon-wrapped scallops, too, but so different from the previous recipe!

32 sea scallops (about a pound)

1/2 cup (120 milliliters) lemon juice

1/2 cup (120 milliliters) sugar-free pancake syrup

Barbecue rub—your choice; Classic Barbecue Rub (page 31) is good here

16 slices bacon

Put your scallops in a bowl. Mix together your lemon juice and pancake syrup and pour it over the scallops. Give them a stir. Then let them marinate for at least a half hour, and a few hours won't hurt—stir them now and again while they marinate.

At least 30 minutes before cooking time, put 4 bamboo skewers in water to soak. Get your grill going before you assemble your kebabs.

Okay, time to make kebabs. With a fork or slotted spoon, lift your scallops out of their marinade. Pat them dry with a paper towel, and put them on a plate. Sprinkle them liberally with the barbecue rub.

Cut your slices of bacon in half. Wrap each scallop around its circumference with a half-slice of bacon, piercing with a bamboo skewer to hold. Put 8 bacon-wrapped scallops on each skewer.

Grill, turning once or twice, over a medium-hot fire—have your water bottle on hand for flare-ups. Baste once or twice with the lemon-maple marinade, but quit with at least 4–5 minutes of cooking to go, to make sure the germs are killed! Cook until the bacon is done and the scallops are fairly firm.

YIELD: 4 servings

If you drank the marinade, you'd get 15 grams of carb per serving, not counting the polyols in the pancake syrup, but you're not going to drink the marinade. I'd give a generous estimate of 5 grams of carbohydrate per serving; 28 grams protein.

chapter eight

Grilled Vegetables and Other Hot Sides

So, there you are, out in the sunshine, having a good time, and there's your main course sizzling away on the grill, smelling like Heaven itself. Who wants to go inside to cook a vegetable to go with the meat? Who wants to risk burning the burgers?

Why bother, when veggies take so well to grilling? Here are a bunch of wonderful, healthy, low-carb sides you can cook without leaving the party.

There are also a few recipes in this chapter that will stick you in the kitchen for a while—but what great recipes! Fried onion rings! Hush puppies! Baked beans! Worth the time in the house, if you ask me, and sure to make you extremely popular when you bear them forth to the ravening hordes on the patio.

Avocado Cream Portobellos

This appetizer is outstandingly delicious and looks elegant on the plate, as well.

> 6 small portobello mushrooms (my grocery store has these
>   under the name Baby Bellas)
> 1/4 cup (60 milliliters) olive oil
> 2 cloves garlic

1 tablespoon dried thyme

2 dashes hot sauce

1 little black avocado

3 tablespoons sour cream

2 tablespoons minced red onion

Salt

6 slices bacon

Remove the stems from your portobellos (save them to slice and sauté for omelets or to serve over steak!) and set the mushroom caps on a plate. Measure the olive oil and crush one of the cloves of garlic into it; then stir in the thyme and the hot sauce. Using a brush, coat the portobello caps on both sides with the olive oil mixture.

Next, cut open your avocado, remove the pit, and scoop it into a small mixing bowl. Mash it with a fork. Stir in the sour cream, the onion, and the other clove of garlic, crushed. Salt the avocado mixture to taste.

Now we have to get your bacon cooking. Lay it on a microwave bacon rack or in a glass pie plate, and nuke it on high for 6 minutes (times may vary a bit depending on the power of your microwave).

While your bacon is cooking, go grill your mushrooms! Lay them on an oiled grill over well-ashed coals, or over a gas grill set to medium to medium-low. Grill for about 7 minutes per side, or until done through, basting frequently with the olive oil mixture—you'll want a water bottle for flare-ups.

When your mushrooms are appealingly grilled, put them back on their plate and march them back to the kitchen. Check your bacon; if it's not crisp, give it another minute or two, then drain it. Divide the avocado mixture between the mushrooms, piling it high in a picturesque fashion. Crumble a slice of bacon over each stuffed mushroom, and serve.

YIELD: 6 appetizer servings

Each will have 9 grams of carbohydrate and 3 grams of fiber, for a usable carb count of 6 grams; 6 grams protein; 701 milligrams of potassium!

☀ Mushroom Bombs

These are so simple, and so wonderful—count on them to disappear in a flash! A *Lowcarbezine!* reader sent in this idea, but sadly, I don't have his or her name. Whoever you are, thank you!

>   1 pound (500 grams) fresh mushrooms
>   2 16-ounce (450-gram) packages bacon (the cheaper the better)

At least 30 minutes before assembling your Mushroom Bombs, start a bunch of wooden toothpicks soaking in water.

Now, get your fire going—you'll want a medium-low fire, since the bacon grease will definitely cause flare-ups.

Wrap each mushroom in a strip of bacon, and anchor it with a toothpick thrust clear through. Wrap all your mushrooms, then set them on the grill. Every few minutes turn the mushrooms, and be sure you have a squirt bottle on hand for those flare-ups! Grill until the bacon is done. Serve as an appetizer, or as a side with a steak.

YIELD: The number of Mushroom Bombs you get will depend on how many mushrooms per pound, of course. Figure this is enough for at least 8 people, and maybe as many as 12, depending on what else you serve.

Assuming 8 people, each will get about 3 grams of carbohydrate and 1 gram of fiber, for a usable carb count of 2 grams; 35 grams of protein, which makes this hearty enough for a main course.

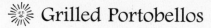 # Grilled Portobellos

4 large portobello mushrooms

1/2 green pepper

1/4 small onion

1 clove garlic, crushed

1/4 cup (60 milliliters) olive oil

Salt and pepper

1/4 cup (25 grams) grated Parmesan cheese

Remove the stems from your portobellos (save them to slice for omelets or to sauté to go on steak) and lay the caps on a plate.

Whack the green pepper and onion both into a few hunks, and put them in your food processor with the S-blade in place. Add the garlic, and pulse until everything is chopped fairly fine. Add the olive oil, and pulse again.

Lay your portobellos gill-side down on a grill over a medium fire, and brush with some of the oil in the green pepper mixture—just dip a brush into it. Let the mushrooms grill for 4–5 minutes. Turn them faceup, and spoon the green pepper and onion mixture into them. Let them grill another 4–5 minutes. Watch for flare-ups from that olive oil! Remove to a serving plate, sprinkle with salt and pepper, and top each mushroom with a tablespoon of Parmesan cheese. Serve.

YIELD: 4 servings

Each serving will have 9 grams of carbohydrate and 2 grams of fiber, for a usable carb count of 7 grams; 6 grams of protein.

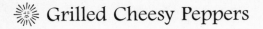 Grilled Cheesy Peppers

A great, easy first course.

>   3 medium green bell peppers
>
>   3 cloves garlic
>
>   3 tablespoons olive oil
>
>   6 ounces (170 grams) Monterey Jack cheese, shredded

Cut the green peppers in half lengthwise, and remove the core and seeds. Crush the garlic, mix it into the olive oil, and brush the insides of the peppers with it. Divide the cheese between the peppers, putting it in the hollows, and spoon the rest of the garlic out of the bottom of the olive oil and divide that between the peppers, too, spooning it over the cheese. Grill over medium coals or a medium gas grill, keeping the lid shut, until the cheese is melted and the peppers softened, then serve.

YIELD: 6 servings

Each serving will have 5 grams of carbohydrate and 1 gram of fiber, for a usable carb count of 4 grams; and 8 grams protein.

 Chipotle Garlic Grilled Asparagus

Wow. Just amazing.

> 2 pounds (1 kilogram) asparagus
> 1 batch Chipotle Garlic Butter (page 57)

Snap off the ends of the asparagus where they break naturally, and make your Chipotle Garlic Butter.

Spoon the Chipotle Garlic Butter into a heatproof container of some sort, and head out toward the grill. Place the Chipotle Garlic Butter close enough to the heat so it will melt, but not burn.

Using a grill basket or a small-holed vegetable grill to keep your asparagus from falling into the fire, grill it, basting frequently with the Chipotle Garlic Butter until it's just tender and getting a few brown spots. Serve.

YIELD: 6–8 servings

Assuming 6 servings, each will have 4 grams of carbohydrate and 2 grams of fiber, for a usable carb count of 2 grams; 2 grams protein.

☀ Grilled Sesame Asparagus

Good with any of the Asian-influenced main courses in this book—or with anything else, for that matter.

    1 pound (500 grams) asparagus

    2 tablespoons soy sauce

    2 tablespoons rice vinegar

    1 tablespoon toasted sesame oil

    1 jalapeno, finely minced

    1 tablespoon sesame seeds

Have your fire ready; the prep on this recipe doesn't take much time.

Snap the bottom off of each stalk of asparagus where it breaks naturally. Mix together the soy sauce, rice vinegar, sesame oil, and minced jalapeno in a bowl. (Now wash your hands! You must always wash your hands after handling hot peppers, or the next time you touch your eyes, nose, or mouth, you'll be sorry.)

Put the sesame seeds in a small, dry skillet, and shake them over a medium-high flame until they start to make little popping sounds. Turn off the burner (and if you have an electric stove, remove the pan from the heat).

Okay, throw your asparagus on the grill, over a medium fire—it's a good idea to have a small-holed grill for this. Baste the asparagus with the soy sauce mixture as it grills, and turn the asparagus a few times. Grill until the asparagus has brown spots, then remove to serving plates. Drizzle with the remaining soy sauce mixture, garnish with the toasted sesame seeds, and serve.

YIELD: 4 servings

Each serving will have 4 grams of carbohydrate and 2 grams of fiber, for a usable carb count of 2 grams; 2 grams protein.

☀ Grilled Broccoli Salad

Before I made this salad, I'd never had grilled broccoli. It's wonderful!

　　1 head broccoli

　　2 tablespoons olive oil

　　1/4 cup (60 milliliters) rice wine vinegar

　　1/4 cup (60 milliliters) soy sauce

　　2 tablespoons toasted sesame oil

　　4 tablespoons sesame seeds

Trim the bottom of the broccoli stem, then cut into spears. Brush with a little of the olive oil, and grill over a medium to medium-low fire until flecked with brown spots. Remove from the fire.

Put the grilled broccoli in a bowl, and add the rest of the oil, the vinegar, the soy sauce, and the sesame oil. Stir everything up, to coat the broccoli, and let the whole thing sit for at least a half hour or so.

Before serving, put your sesame seeds in a small, dry skillet, and shake them over a medium-high flame until they start to make little popping sounds. Add to your salad, toss, and serve at room temperature.

YIELD: 4–5 servings

Assuming 4, each will have 12 grams of carbohydrate and 6 grams of fiber, for a usable carb count of 6 grams; 7 grams protein.

About Grilled Zucchini

Before offering the next few recipes—especially good choices for National Sneak a Zucchini onto Your Neighbor's Front Porch Week—I'd like to point out that I've specified smallish zucchinis only because I think they look nice. If you've got big zucchinis, feel free to cut them up! You can also use yellow summer squash in these recipes, should you prefer.

Easy Grilled Zucchini

> 6 smallish zucchinis
>
> ¹/₂ cup (120 milliliters) bottled Italian dressing (not creamy style)

Split your zukes lengthwise, and cut off the stems. Put them in a big zipper-lock bag and pour the dressing over them. Press the air out of the bag, seal it, and turn it over a few times to coat the zucchinis. Now stash them in the fridge until dinner.

When suppertime rolls around, pull out the bag, pour off the dressing into a bowl or pan, and throw the zucchinis on the grill. Baste them with the dressing, and grill them until they're getting soft, with brown stripes; then serve.

YIELD: 6 servings

If you consumed all the salad dressing, each serving would have 8 grams of carbohydrate and 2 grams of fiber, but you'll discard most of the dressing. Figure closer to 4 grams of carbohydrate per serving, with those same 2 grams of fiber, for a usable carb count of around 2 grams per serving; 2 grams protein.

☀ Lemon-Garlic Grilled Zucchini

Sunny summer flavor!

6 smallish zucchinis

1/2 cup (120 milliliters) olive oil

1/4 cup (60 milliliters) lemon juice

2 cloves garlic, crushed

Salt and pepper

Split your zucchinis in half lengthwise, and cut off the stems. Put them in a large zipper-lock bag. Mix together the olive oil, lemon juice, and garlic, and pour the mixture into the bag. Press out the air, seal the bag, turn it a few times to coat the zukes, and throw it in the fridge until you need it.

When grilling time comes, pull out the bag, pour off the marinade into a bowl, and throw your zukes on the grill. Baste them with the lemon dressing, and grill them until they're getting soft, with brown grill marks. Salt and pepper them, and serve.

YIELD: 6 servings

With the marinade, this comes to 7 grams of carbohydrate per serving, and 2 grams of fiber, but you'll discard much of that. I'd say 4 grams of carbohydrate, with those 2 grams of fiber, for a usable carb count of 2 grams; 2 grams protein.

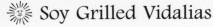 Soy Grilled Vidalias

I'm always so torn about onions. On the one hand, they're higher carb than most vegetables. On the other hand, they're extremely nutritious and taste incredibly good—and certainly aren't as high carb as, say, a potato. So I grill onions, but I watch my portions.

> 2 large Vidalia onions
>
> 1/4 cup (60 milliliters) soy sauce
>
> 1 clove garlic, crushed
>
> 2 teaspoons Splenda

Peel your onions and slice them pretty thickly—about 1/2" (1.25 centimeters) or a little thicker. Mix together everything else. Lay your onion slices in a grill basket, or on a small-holed grill rack over a medium fire. Baste them with the soy sauce mixture, and grill them until they're limp, with brown spots; then serve.

Note: You may well find that your slices fall apart into individual rings when you turn them. This doesn't bother me, but if it bothers you, here's a trick: before slicing your onions, pierce them with wooden or bamboo skewers (soak them in water for at least a half hour first) a half-inch apart, then slice between the skewers. Your slices will come out neatly skewered across the rings, for easy turning.

YIELD: If you can bring yourself to share these between 6 people, each of you will get 4 grams of carbohydrate and 1 gram of fiber, for a usable carb count of 3 grams; 1 gram protein.

 Balsamic Grilled Vidalias

2 large Vidalia onions

1/4 cup (60 milliliters) bottled balsamic vinaigrette dressing

Peel your onions and slice them about 1/2" (1.25 centimeters) thick—if you like, you can do the trick with the skewers in the Soy Grilled Vidalias recipe (page 180), to hold the slices together on the grill. Put your dressing in a small bowl, and haul everything out to the grill.

Now, lay the onion slices in a grill basket or on a small-holed grill rack, over a medium fire. Grill them, basting frequently with the dressing, until they're limp, with brown spots; then serve.

YIELD: 6 servings

Each serving will have 3 grams of carbohydrate and 1 gram of fiber, for a usable carb count of 2 grams; a trace of protein.

☀ Grilled Radicchio with Balsamic Vinaigrette

The grilling mellows the bitter edge of the radicchio, and the balsamic vinegar complements and enhances its newfound sweetness. I really love this!

1/4 cup (60 milliliters) olive oil

2 tablespoons balsamic vinegar

1 clove garlic

1 dash salt

1 dash pepper

1 head radicchio

Mix together everything but the radicchio. Now, trim just the very bottom of the radicchio's stem, and cut the whole thing in quarters from top to bottom (you want a bit of stem in each quarter, holding it together). Put the radicchio quarters on a plate, and spoon some of the balsamic vinaigrette over them, letting it drizzle down between the leaves.

Now grill your radicchio, turning once or twice, until it's going limp and starting to brown; then serve, drizzling it with a little more vinaigrette if you like.

YIELD: 4 servings

Each serving will have 1 gram of carbohydrate and a trace of fiber, and a trace of protein.

☀ Hobo Packet

Cooks right on the grill along with your meat course—not even a mixing bowl to wash! Really tasty, too.

- 1/2 head cauliflower
- 1/2 medium onion
- 1 medium carrot
- 1 large rib celery
- 1/2 teaspoon salt
- 1/2 teaspoon pepper
- 8 slices bacon, cooked
- 2 tablespoons butter

Chop your cauliflower into smallish chunks. Coarsely chop the onion, slice the carrot about 1/4" (1 centimeter) thick, and slice the celery about the same thickness.

Tear off a piece of heavy-duty aluminum foil about 18" (45 centimeters) long, and lay it on the counter. Pile the vegetables in the middle. Salt and pepper them, crumble the cooked bacon on top, and dot the whole thing with the butter. Fold the foil over the whole thing, and fold the seam a few times to seal it well. Roll up the ends to seal them, too.

Throw the whole packet on the grill, and give it about 12–15 minutes per side over a medium charcoal fire or gas grill. Pull the packet off the grill with tongs, put it on a plate to open it up, and serve.

YIELD: 6 servings

Each serving will have 3 grams of carbohydrate and 1 gram of fiber, for a usable carb count of 2 grams; 3 grams protein.

☀ Cheesy Veggie Packet

See all those halves? Think it might be easy to double this recipe, hmmm? And who doesn't like vegetables with melted cheese?

1/2 head cauliflower

1/2 medium onion

1/2 green bell pepper

2 tablespoons butter

Salt and pepper

1/2 cup (60 grams) shredded cheddar cheese

Trim the stem on your cauliflower, but don't bother to core it. Whack it into chunks. Chop your onion, and dice your pepper. Tear off a big piece of heavy-duty foil, and pile your veggies in the center—jumble them up so they'll flavor each other. Now, cut the butter into little chunks and dot it over the vegetables, and salt and pepper them a bit. Strew the cheese over the whole thing. Now fold opposite sides of the foil to the center and roll down, making a tight seam. Roll up the ends. Throw the whole thing on the grill over medium heat, and let it cook for 10–12 minutes. Flip the packet over with tongs and give it another 10–12 minutes, then serve.

YIELD: 3–4 servings

Assuming 4, each will have 3 grams of carbohydrate and 1 gram of fiber, for a usable carb count of 2 grams; 4 grams protein.

☀ Balsamic Veggie Packet

My husband, no big fan of summer squash, really liked this.

> 2 medium turnips, peeled and cut into strips
>
> 1/2 medium onion, sliced
>
> 1 medium yellow summer squash, halved lengthwise and sliced
>   (substitute zucchini, if you prefer)
>
> 1 cup (225 grams) broccoli florets
>
> 1/4 cup (60 milliliters) olive oil
>
> 1 clove garlic, crushed
>
> 2 tablespoons balsamic vinegar
>
> Salt and pepper

You'll need a big piece of heavy-duty foil. When you've got your vegetables cut up, heap them in the center of a piece of foil, jumbling them together. Mix the oil, garlic, and balsamic vinegar together. Making sure that the edges of the foil are turned up a bit, drizzle this mixture over the vegetables. Salt and pepper the whole thing. Then bring opposite sides of the foil together and roll down to make a strong seam. Roll up the ends. Throw the whole thing on a medium grill for 12 minutes per side, then serve.

YIELD: 5–6 servings

Assuming 5, each will have 7 grams of carbohydrate and 2 grams of fiber, for a usable carb count of 5 grams; 1 gram protein.

☀ Hush Puppies

I didn't know how this would work out, but it turned out very well indeed! You'll need a deep-fat fryer, or at least a deep, heavy kettle and a frying thermometer. My thanks to my Alabaman friend Kay, for helping me get this recipe right. (She also tells me, a bit late, that hush puppies really go with fish fries, but hey, I got the idea from *Southern Living* magazine. I'm a Yankee, what do I know?)

2/3 cup (80 grams) Atkins Cornbread Mix

2 tablespoons Atkins Bake Mix

1/4 cup (30 grams) rice protein powder

1 teaspoon seasoned salt

1/2 cup (120 milliliters) canola oil

1/2 cup (120 milliliters) water

2 eggs

1/4 cup (40 grams) finely minced onion

Start your deep-fat fryer heating to 370°F (190°C).

In a medium-sized mixing bowl, stir the Atkins Cornbread Mix, Atkins Bake Mix, rice protein powder, and salt together. In a 2-cup glass measure, measure the oil, then the water (so that together, the level is 1 cup). Break the eggs into the oil-and-water mixture, and whisk the whole combination together. Stir the onion into the liquid ingredients. Then pour into the dry ingredients, and stir the whole thing together with a few big strokes, just until everything's wet—don't overmix.

When your oil is up to temperature, drop the batter into the hot fat by the table-spoonful, and fry until golden, just a few minutes. Drain on absorbent paper, and serve hot.

YIELD: 6 servings, at least!

Assuming 6, each serving will have 12 grams of carbohydrate and 3 grams of fiber, for a usable carb count of 9 grams; 17 grams of protein. (By comparison, a 5-pup serving of restaurant hush puppies will generally contain about 35 grams of carbohydrate.)

☀ Unbelievable Onion Rings

The thing you'll find hard to believe is that these are far lower carb than the high-carb onion rings you get at restaurants! They're not dirt-low in carbs, but to me, onion rings are crack in food form, so being able to have a really good, reasonably low-carb onion ring now and then is a very big deal.

3 medium Vidalia onions

1 cup (120 grams) Atkins Bake Mix

2 tablespoons Atkins Cornbread Mix

1/4 cup (30 grams) oat flour

1 teaspoon seasoned salt

2 eggs

12 ounces (360 milliliters) light beer (Michelob Ultra, Miller Lite,
    or Milwaukee's Best Light are lowest carb)

Start your deep-fat fryer heating to 375°F (190°C).

Peel the onions and slice them fairly thick. Separate them into rings, and set aside.

In a medium-sized mixing bowl, combine the Atkins Bake Mix, Atkins Cornbread Mix, oat flour, and seasoned salt, stirring them together well. Add the eggs and the beer, and whisk them in.

When the fat is up to temperature, dip the onion rings into the batter, then drop them (carefully!) into the hot fat. (Note: If you're using a deep-fat fryer, have your fry basket already submerged. If you put the batter-coated rings in the basket, then lower it, your onion rings will weld themselves to your fry basket and create a royal mess.) Fry until golden (you may have to turn them over to get both sides browned), drain on absorbent paper, salt, and devour!

YIELD: 6 servings

14 grams of carbohydrate and 4 grams of fiber, for a usable carb count of 10 grams; 16 grams of protein. (By comparison, a serving of 8–9 restaurant onion rings averages about 30 grams of carbohydrate.)

☼ Low-Carb BBQ Baked Beans

In many parts of the country, baked beans are an indispensable side dish with any barbecue. Sadly, most beans are way too high carbohydrate for us. However, there is one sort of bean that is low-enough carb for us: black soybeans. You'll want to buy them canned, because soybeans take forever to cook soft—you can find them at the health food store; a company called Eden cans them. They're sort of bland by themselves, but add onions, celery, et cetera, et cetera, et cetera, and they're fabulous. These aren't actually baked, I admit. I trust you'll forgive me. This makes only 4 servings, but it's very easy to double.

3 slices bacon

1/4 cup (40 grams) minced onion

1/4 cup (40 grams) minced celery

1/4 cup (40 grams) finely chopped green bell pepper

1 15-ounce (420-gram) can black soybeans

3 tablespoons Dana's No-Sugar Ketchup (page 30)

2 tablespoons Splenda

1/2 teaspoon blackstrap molasses

1 dash salt

1 dash pepper

1 dash hot sauce

Chop up your bacon, or snip it right into a saucepan with your kitchen shears. Start it cooking over medium heat. When some grease has cooked out of your bacon, add the onion, celery, and green pepper. Sauté the vegetables in the bacon grease until soft.

Drain the canned black soybeans, and dump them in with the vegetables. Stir in the ketchup, Splenda, molasses, salt, pepper, and hot sauce. Turn the burner to low, cover, and let the whole thing simmer for 15 minutes or so, then serve.

YIELD: 4 servings

Each serving will have 11 grams of carbohydrate and 6 grams of fiber, for a usable carb count of 5 grams; 11 grams protein. (Bush's brand Barbecue Baked Beans have 32 grams of carbohydrate in a 1/2-cup serving!)

chapter nine

Salads, Slaws, and Other Cold Sides

Fresh, crisp, delicious, and overwhelmingly nutritious, salads or raw vegetables with a tasty dip are the very best foil for a hot, rich, and spicy slab of barbecued anything! Indeed, for many people, it's just not a cookout without a bowl of coleslaw or maybe a scoop of potato salad, or both. Sadly, most coleslaw recipes are full of sugar, and potatoes are out if we want to keep our waistlines, not to mention stable blood sugar.

No worries! Here you'll find lots of new ways with coleslaw, and "unpotato" salads that will drive all longing for the "real thing" clear out of your mind. These aren't the only make-ahead salads—you'll find several you can make in advance and stash in the fridge until dinnertime. New dips, too, to serve with that relish tray, and new ways with tossed salads. Even sweet, spicy, and sugar-free bread-and-butter pickles to go with that burger!

So enjoy summer's garden bounty. There's nothing better with a slab of ribs or a pile of grilled chicken!

☀ Avocado Ranch Dip

Serve this way-simple dip with celery sticks, pepper strips, and cucumber rounds while the meat is grilling, and you can skip the salad. You can use this as a rather thick salad dressing, if you prefer.

> 1 cup (225 milliliters) bottled ranch salad dressing
>
> 2 little black avocados
>
> 1 tablespoon lime juice
>
> 1 dash Tabasco sauce

Put the ranch dressing in your blender or food processor, and scoop in the flesh of one of your avocados. Add the lime juice and Tabasco, and process until smooth. Scoop the other avocado into the bowl you plan to serve the dip in, and mash it fairly coarsely with a fork—you want some small chunks of avocado in your dip. Scrape the mixture out of the blender or processor into the bowl, stir to blend the mashed avocado into the pureed mixture, and serve.

Note: Like anything made with avocado, this is prone to changing color on standing, so don't make it in advance. It's not like it takes a lot of time or anything. If you have leftovers—I sure didn't!—smooth a piece of plastic wrap onto the surface of the dip before refrigerating to prevent exposure to air.

YIELD: Makes roughly 2 cups, or 8 servings of 1/4 cup each.

5 grams of carbohydrate and 2 grams of fiber, for a usable carb count of 3 grams; 2 grams protein; 288 milligrams potassium!

☀ Blue~Green Guacamole

Have you figured out yet that I'm crazy for avocados? They're incredibly good for you, and are the best low-carb source of potassium, so eat them often! Adding blue cheese and olives to this guacamole really gives it an exciting new twist.

2 little black avocados

1/3 cup (40 grams) crumbled blue cheese

1/4 cup (60 grams) sour cream

1/4 cup (25 grams) chopped black olives

2 cloves garlic

1/4 teaspoon Tabasco sauce

1 1/2 teaspoons lime juice

Salt and pepper

Halve your avocados, remove the pits, and scoop them into a mixing bowl. Mash them coarsely with a fork. Stir in everything through the lime juice, salt and pepper it to taste, and serve with vegetable dippers or low-carb tortilla chips.

Note: Anything made with avocados will turn brown on you after being exposed to air for a while, and it sure does look unappealing. So don't make your guac in advance, and if you have leftovers, smooth a piece of plastic wrap right onto the surface of the leftover guacamole to seal out air.

YIELD: 6 servings

Each serving will have 5 grams of carbohydrate and 3 grams of fiber, for a usable carb count of 2 grams; 3 grams protein; 405 milligrams potassium!

☀ Spicy Tuna Dip

When I served this at a big barbecue, people were jokingly fighting over it! This would also make a great take-along lunch—a container of dip and a baggie of cut-up veggies, and you're good to go!

1/2 cup (120 grams) plain yogurt

1/2 cup (120 grams) mayonnaise

6 ounces (140 grams) canned tuna in water, drained

1/4 small red onion, chopped

2 teaspoons chili garlic paste

1/2 teaspoon xanthan or guar

Just plunk everything in your food processor with the S-blade in place, and process till smooth. Serve with vegetable dippers.

YIELD: 8 servings

Each serving will have 1 gram of carbohydrate and a trace of fiber; 5 grams protein.

Slaws

Feel like it just isn't a barbecue without slaw? Here are a cool half dozen slaw recipes, from classic creamy coleslaw to an exotic Spicy Peanut Slaw, and unlike the vast majority of coleslaw recipes, these have no sugar. Cabbage never looked so good!

☀ Classic Coleslaw

This is a repeat from *500 Low-Carb Recipes*—it's simply the best classic creamy coleslaw recipe I've ever come up with, so I figured I'd throw it in.

> 1 head green cabbage, or 7 cups bagged coleslaw mix
>
> 1/4 red onion
>
> 1/2 cup (120 grams) mayonnaise
>
> 1/2 cup (120 grams) sour cream
>
> 1–1 1/2 tablespoons cider vinegar
>
> 1–1 1/2 teaspoons prepared mustard
>
> 1/2–1 teaspoon salt or Vege-Sal
>
> 1/2 –1 packet artificial sweetener, or 1 teaspoon Splenda

Using a food processor's slicing blade or a sharp knife, reduce your cabbage to little bitty shreds, and put those shreds in a great big bowl. Mince the onion really fine, and put that in the bowl, too.

Mix together everything else, blending well. Pour over the cabbage and onion, and toss well. You can serve this right away, if you like, but it improves with at least a few hours' worth of refrigeration.

YIELD: 10 servings

Each serving will have 1 gram of carbohydrate, a trace of fiber, and 1 gram of protein.

☀ Bayou Slaw

I've never been a fan of "vinegar slaw" before, but this one changed my mind. Addictive! Sweet and tart and spicy.

6 cups (450 grams) shredded cabbage (1 modest-sized head of cabbage,
   or use bagged coleslaw mix if you like)

1/2 green pepper, cut in matchstick strips

3 scallions sliced thin, including the crisp part of the green shoot

1/3 cup (80 milliliters) red wine vinegar

1/3 cup (80 milliliters) olive oil

2 tablespoons Splenda

1 teaspoon onion powder

1 teaspoon salt

1 teaspoon dry mustard

1/2 teaspoon celery salt

1/2 teaspoon Tabasco sauce

Plunk your vegetables into a good-sized mixing bowl. Then mix together everything else, pour it over the slaw, and toss. This is great right away, but like most slaws, it improves with 12 hours' to a day's standing.

YIELD: 6 servings

Each serving will have 7 grams of carbohydrate and 2 grams of fiber, for a usable carb count of 5 grams; and 1 gram of protein.

☀ Lemon Slaw

The lemon flavor in this slaw makes it a natural with grilled fish, seafood, or poultry. And the combination of vegetables makes it appealingly colorful!

1/2 head cabbage, shredded, or 4 cups (300 grams) bagged coleslaw mix

1 green pepper, cut in matchstick strips

1/2 cup (80 grams) diced red onion

1 small carrot, shredded

4 tablespoons chopped fresh parsley

1/2 cup (120 grams) mayonnaise

1/2 cup (120 grams) plain yogurt

1/4 cup (60 milliliters) lemon juice

2 tablespoons olive oil

1 tablespoon white wine vinegar

1/2 teaspoon pepper

2 tablespoons Dijon mustard

1 tablespoon Splenda

1 tablespoon prepared horseradish

1/2 teaspoon celery seed

Combine your veggies, through the parsley, in a big mixing bowl. Then whisk together everything else, pour your dressing over the cabbage mixture, and toss well. Chill for at least a few hours before serving.

YIELD: 6 servings

Each serving will have 7 grams of carbohydrate and 2 grams of fiber, for a usable carb count of 5 grams; 2 grams protein.

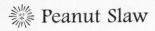 Peanut Slaw

Peanuts in slaw sound odd? It's actually remarkably good.

    1 head cabbage, shredded, or 7 cups (525 grams) bagged coleslaw mix.

    8 scallions sliced thin, including the crisp part of the green shoot

    1 cup (240 grams) mayonnaise

    1 tablespoon Splenda

    1/8 teaspoon blackstrap molasses

    2 tablespoons toasted sesame oil

    1/2 cup (75 grams) dry-roasted peanuts, chopped

Put your cabbage in a big mixing bowl, and add the scallions. Stir together the mayo, Splenda, blackstrap, and toasted sesame oil; pour the dressing over the vegetables, and toss. Add the peanuts, and toss again.

YIELD: 8 servings

Each serving will have 4 grams of carbohydrate and 1 gram of fiber, for a usable carb count of 3 grams; 3 grams protein.

✺ Spicy Peanut Slaw

I like peanuts in my coleslaw. Does it show? The chili garlic paste gives this a kick that sets it apart from the Peanut Slaw (page 196).

  1 head cabbage, shredded, or 7 cups (525 grams) bagged coleslaw mix

  8 scallions sliced

  1 cup (240 grams) mayonnaise

  1 tablespoon Splenda

  1/8 teaspoon blackstrap molasses

  2 teaspoons chili garlic paste

  1/2 cup (75 grams) chopped dry-roasted peanuts

Follow directions for Peanut Slaw (facing page), adding in chili garlic paste with mayo, Splenda, and blackstrap molasses.

YIELD: 8 servings

Each serving will have 4 grams of carbohydrate and 1 gram of fiber, for a usable carb count of 3 grams; 3 grams protein.

☀ Sesame Slaw

A big hit at our annual Toastmaster's Bash by the Lake. Wonderful with anything with an Asian accent. This is not only low carb, but very low calorie, as well.

1 head cabbage, shredded, or 7 cups (525 grams) bagged coleslaw mix.

3 scallions, sliced thin, including the crisp part of the green shoot

1 cup (50 grams) bean sprouts

5 ounces (140 grams) canned water chestnuts, chopped

1 bunch cilantro, chopped

2 tablespoons sesame seeds

2 teaspoons grated gingerroot

1/4 cup (60 milliliters) lime juice

3 tablespoons soy sauce

2 teaspoons Splenda

In a big mixing bowl combine the cabbage, scallions, bean sprouts, water chestnuts, and cilantro.

Put your sesame seeds in a small, heavy, dry skillet, and shake them over a high flame until they start to make popping noises. Turn off the burner and set the sesame seeds aside.

Combine everything else, pour it over the vegetables, and toss. Add the toasted sesame seeds, and toss again. Chill for a few hours before serving.

YIELD: 8 servings

Each serving will have 6 grams of carbohydrate and 1 gram of fiber, for a usable carb count of 5 grams; 2 grams protein.

☀ Sauerkraut Salad

Unusual! This salad has the advantage of using mostly stuff that keeps well—so you just might have the ingredients hanging around the house when you discover that the head of lettuce you bought last week has gone south.

2 cups (280 grams) sauerkraut, rinsed

1/2 green bell pepper

1 large rib celery

1/4 medium red onion

1/4 cup (60 milliliters) Splenda

2 tablespoons cider vinegar

2 tablespoons oil

Rinse your sauerkraut and put it in a bowl. Slice your pepper into matchstick strips, and thinly slice your celery and onion; add all the vegetables to the sauerkraut. Now, add the Splenda, cider vinegar, and oil; toss; and stick the bowl in the fridge. Let the whole thing marinate for a few hours before serving.

YIELD: 4–5 servings

Assuming 5, each will have 7 grams of carbohydrate and 3 grams of fiber, for a usable carb count of 4 grams; 1 gram protein.

UnPotato Salads

Potato salad is another one of those must-have dishes for barbecues and cookouts, but it's hard to think of anything that's more off-limits for the low-carb dieter. Well, my friend, just wait till you try making "potato" salad with cauliflower. You'll be amazed! Here's a heckuva selection to try.

☀ UnPotato Salad

Another recipe borrowed from *500 Low-Carb Recipes*. This is astonishingly like real potato salad.

> 1 large head cauliflower
>
> 2 cups (320 grams) diced celery
>
> 1 cup (160 grams) diced red onion
>
> 2 cups (480 grams) mayonnaise
>
> 1/4 cup (60 milliliters) cider vinegar
>
> 2 teaspoons salt or Vege-Sal
>
> 2 teaspoons Splenda
>
> 1/2 teaspoon pepper
>
> 4 hard-boiled eggs, coarsely chopped

Cut your cauliflower into 1/2" (1.25-centimeter) chunks—don't bother to core it, just cut up the core, too. Put your cauliflower in a microwave-safe casserole, add just a tablespoon or so of water, and cover. Cook it on high for 7 minutes, and let it sit, covered, for another 3–5 minutes. You want your cauliflower tender, but not mushy. (You may steam your cauliflower if you prefer.)

Drain the cooked cauliflower, and combine it with the celery and onion. (You'll need a big bowl.)

Combine the mayonnaise, vinegar, salt, Splenda, and pepper. Pour the mixture over the vegetables, and mix well. Mix in the chopped eggs last and stir only lightly, to preserve some small hunks of yolk. Chill and serve.

YIELD: 12 servings

Each serving will have 3 grams of carbohydrate and 1 gram of fiber, for a total of 2 grams of usable carb; 3 grams of protein.

☀ Garden UnPotato Salad

Beautiful, creamy, and delicious.

1/2 head cauliflower

1/2 cup (40 grams) snow pea pods, fresh, cut in 1/2" (1.25-centimeter) lengths

1/2 medium carrot, grated

1/4 cup (40 grams) diced red bell pepper

1/4 cup (40 grams) diced green bell pepper

1/4 cup (40 grams) diced celery

1/4 cup (40 grams) diced red onion

3 hard-boiled eggs, coarsely chopped

1/4 cup (60 milliliters) heavy cream

1/2 cup (120 grams) mayonnaise

2 teaspoons finely chopped low-carb Bread and Butter Pickles (page 214)

2 teaspoons Dijon mustard

Salt and pepper

4 tablespoons chopped fresh dill weed

First, cut your cauliflower into 1/2" (1.25-centimer) chunks—don't bother coring it first, just trim the bottom of the stem and cut up the core with the rest of it. Put your cauliflower chunks in a microwavable casserole with a lid, add a few table-spoons of water, and nuke it on high for 7 minutes.

When the cauliflower comes out of the microwave, put your cut-up snow peas in a small microwavable bowl, cover with plastic wrap or a saucer, and microwave on high for just a minute. Drain the cauliflower and put it in a large mixing bowl, and add all the other vegetables (including the snow peas you just nuked) and the eggs.

In a medium-sized bowl, mix together the cream and mayonnaise. Stir in the chopped pickle and mustard, and pour the dressing over the vegetables. Mix well, then salt and pepper to taste. Stir in the fresh dill, and chill for 1–2 hours before serving.

YIELD: 6 servings

Each serving will have 4 grams of carbohydrate and 1 gram of fiber, for a usable carb count of 3 grams; 4 grams protein.

German UnPotato Salad

My husband doesn't care for potato salad, but he likes this. Must be his Germanic blood. Or, just as likely, the bacon!

 1/2 head cauliflower

 8 slices bacon

 1/2 medium onion, chopped

 2 tablespoons cider vinegar

 1/2 cup (120 milliliters) water

 1 teaspoon salt

 2 teaspoons Splenda

 Guar or xanthan

First cut your cauliflower into 1/2" (1.25-centimeter) chunks—don't bother coring it first, just trim the bottom of the stem and cut up the core with the rest of it. Put your cauliflower chunks in a microwavable casserole with a lid, add a few table-spoons of water, and nuke it on high for 7 minutes.

While that's happening, snip your bacon into a skillet with kitchen shears, or chop it up and throw it in a skillet. Either way, cook your little bits of bacon until they're starting to get crisp. Throw in the onion, and let it cook a couple of minutes. Then stir in the vinegar, water, salt, and Splenda, and let the whole thing simmer for a couple of minutes more.

Somewhere in here, your microwave will have beeped. Pull out your cauliflower, drain it, and dump it into a mixing bowl. Now, thicken up the mixture in the skillet a little with your guar or xanthan shaker, then scrape it over the cauliflower, and mix well. We like this served hot, but you can serve it at room temperature if you prefer.

YIELD: 4 servings

Each serving will have 3 grams of carbohydrate and 1 gram of fiber, for a usable carb count of 2 grams; 4 grams protein.

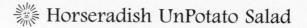 # Horseradish UnPotato Salad

¹/₂ head cauliflower

3 scallions, sliced, including the crisp part of the green shoot

2 tablespoons chopped fresh parsley

¹/₄ cup (60 grams) sour cream

¹/₄ cup (60 grams) plain yogurt

¹/₄ cup (60 grams) mayonnaise

1 tablespoon prepared horseradish

Salt and pepper

First, cut your cauliflower into ¹/₂" (1.25-centimeter) chunks—don't bother coring it first, just trim the bottom of the stem and cut up the core with the rest of it. Put your cauliflower chunks in a microwavable casserole with a lid, add a few tablespoons of water, and nuke it on high for 7 minutes.

When the cauliflower is done, drain it and put it in a mixing bowl. Add the scallions and parsley. Then stir together everything else except the salt and pepper, pour over the vegetables, and mix well. Salt and pepper to taste; then chill for at least a few hours before serving.

YIELD: 4 servings

Each serving will have 3 grams of carbohydrate and 1 gram of fiber, for a usable carb count of 2 grams; 2 grams protein.

 Austin UnPotato Salad

The original potato salad recipe I started with and adapted into this (extremely yummy!) cauliflower salad was credited to Laura Bush, back when she was First Lady of Texas—hence the name. This spicy salad is a natural with barbecued beef brisket or beef ribs.

    1/2 head cauliflower

    1 medium jalapeno pepper

    1/4 cup (25 grams) chopped kalamata olives

    1 tablespoon spicy brown mustard

    1/2 cup (120 grams) mayonnaise

    4 tablespoons chopped cilantro

First, cut your cauliflower into 1/2" (1.25-centimeter) chunks—don't bother coring it first, just trim the bottom of the stem and cut up the core with the rest of it. Put your cauliflower chunks in a microwavable casserole with a lid, add a few table-spoons of water, and nuke it on high for 7 minutes.

When your cauliflower is done, drain it and put it in a large mixing bowl. Halve your jalapeno, seed it, mince it fine, and add it to the cauliflower, then wash your hands. If your kalamata olives have pits in them, you'll need to remove those; then chop up the olives a bit further and throw them in, too.

Mix together the mustard and mayonnaise, pour this dressing over the salad, and mix well. Stir in the chopped cilantro, and chill for a few hours before serving.

YIELD: 4 servings

Each serving will have 2 grams of carbohydrate and 1 gram of fiber, for a usable carb count of 1 gram; 1 gram protein.

☀ Southwestern UnPotato Salad

Of all the unpotato salads I've come up with for this book, this one is my favorite!

- 1/2 head cauliflower
- 1/2 cup (120 grams) mayonnaise
- 2 tablespoons spicy mustard
- 1 tablespoon lime juice
- 1 small jalapeno
- 1/2 cup (30 grams) chopped cilantro
- 1 clove garlic, crushed
- 1/2 cup (40 grams) diced red onion
- 1 small tomato

First, cut your cauliflower into 1/2" (1.25-centimeter) chunks—don't bother coring it first, just trim the bottom of the stem and cut up the core with the rest of it. Put your cauliflower chunks in a microwavable casserole with a lid, add a few table-spoons of water, and nuke it on high for 7 minutes.

When your cauliflower is done, drain it and put it in a large mixing bowl. In a medium-sized bowl, whisk together the mayo, mustard, and lime juice; then pour it over the cauliflower and mix well.

Cut the jalapeno in half, remove the seeds, and mince it fine. Add it to the salad along with the cilantro, garlic, and diced red onion (don't forget to wash your hands!); mix again.

Finally, cut the stem out of the tomato and cut the tomato into smallish dice, then carefully stir it in. Chill the salad for a few hours before serving.

YIELD: 6 servings

Each serving will have 3 grams of carbohydrate and 1 gram of fiber, for a usable carb count of 2 grams; 1 gram protein.

☀ Curried Cauliflower Salad

I think this would be great with grilled or barbecued lamb, myself.

> 1/2 head cauliflower
>
> 5 scallions
>
> 4 hard-boiled eggs
>
> 1/2 cup (120 grams) mayonnaise
>
> 1 tablespoon spicy brown mustard
>
> 1 teaspoon curry powder
>
> 1 dash salt
>
> 1 dash pepper

Chop your cauliflower, including the trimmed stem, into 1/2" (1.25-centimeter) bits. Put it in a microwavable casserole with a lid, add a couple of tablespoons of water, cover, and nuke it on high for 7 minutes.

Meanwhile, slice your scallions, including the crisp part of the green, and chop up your hard-boiled eggs. Next, measure the mayonnaise, mustard, curry powder, salt, and pepper into a bowl, and whisk them together.

Okay, the cauliflower is done now! Drain it, put it in a mixing bowl, and pour the dressing over it. Stir it up well so the cauliflower is coated with the dressing. When it's had a chance to cool a little, add the scallions and eggs and stir it up again. Refrigerate until a half hour before dinner, but remove from the fridge and let it warm up a little before serving—this is good at room temperature.

YIELD: 4–5 servings

Assuming 4, each will have 3 grams of carbohydrate, with 1 gram of fiber, for a usable carb count of 2 grams; 8 grams protein.

☀ Bean Salad with Hot Bacon Dressing

I've used canned beans in this recipe because I can't get fresh or frozen wax beans hereabouts. (I can, of course, get green beans in any form you can imagine.) If you can find fresh or frozen wax beans, however, I bet they'd be better than the canned. Just cut 'em up and cook 'em till they're just tender, and proceed from there.

- 5 slices bacon
- 2 tablespoons Splenda
- 1/2 teaspoon salt or Vege-Sal
- 1/4 teaspoon pepper
- 3 tablespoons distilled vinegar
- 1 15-ounce (420-gram) can green beans
- 1 15-ounce (420-gram) can wax beans

First, cook your bacon: lay it on a microwave bacon rack or in a glass pie plate and microwave on high for 5 minutes or until crisp. Drain, pouring 1 1/2 tablespoons of the bacon grease into a saucepan. Warm the saucepan over low heat.

Add the Splenda, salt or Vege-Sal, pepper, and vinegar to the bacon grease, and whisk this mixture together. Let this simmer on low heat for a minute while you open your two cans of beans and drain them. Dump the beans into a salad bowl, crumble the bacon over them, pour the hot dressing over them, toss, and serve.

YIELD: 5–6 servings

Assuming 6, each will have 7 grams of carbohydrate and 2 grams of fiber, for a usable carb count of 5 grams; 3 grams protein.

☀ Artichoke Prosciutto Salad

This salad is rich, and more filling than some others in this book. Serve it with a lighter grilled dish—maybe a seafood kebab or grilled chicken.

1 14-ounce (400-gram) can artichoke hearts, drained

2 ounces (60 grams) prosciutto or good-quality deli ham, thinly sliced

1/2 cup (50 grams) chopped kalamata olives

1 medium tomato

4 tablespoons chopped fresh basil

3 tablespoons extra virgin olive oil

1 tablespoon white wine vinegar

1 clove garlic

1/2 teaspoon Dijon mustard

1 teaspoon Splenda

Coarsely chop the artichoke hearts and throw them into a mixing bowl. Cut the prosciutto or ham into strips about 1" (2.5 centimeters) long and 1/4" (1 centimeter) wide, and throw that in, too. Chop the olives and add them; then dice the tomato and put that in, too. Finally, throw in the chopped fresh basil.

Mix together everything else and pour it over the vegetables. Stir up the whole thing. Let it marinate for several hours before serving.

YIELD: 4 servings

Each serving will have 10 grams carbohydrate and 1 gram fiber, for a usable carb count of 9 grams—but a lot of the fiber in artichokes is in the form of inulin, which has a very low glycemic index, so this is considerably easier on your blood sugar than that 9-gram figure would suggest. 7 grams protein.

☀ Seven Layer Salad

This salad is a '70s throwback; my mom used to make a version of this for dinner parties. This reduced-carb version is just as good as the original—and gives you a green salad you can make in advance, which is very convenient for parties.

8 ounces (230 grams) snow peas

12 ounces (340 grams) bagged mixed salad greens

1 medium green pepper

2 ribs celery

1/2 medium red onion

1 cup (240 grams) mayonnaise

1/2 cup (120 grams) sour cream

1/2 cup (120 milliliters) ranch salad dressing

1 tablespoon Splenda

6 slices bacon, cooked crisp and crumbled

3/4 cup (90 grams) shredded cheddar cheese

This salad is best made in a large, clear glass bowl, to show off the layers.

First, you need to prep your snow peas: cut off the ends, pull off any tough strings, and cut them into 1/2" (1.25-centimeter) lengths. Put the snow peas in a microwavable bowl, add a tablespoon or so of water, cover with plastic wrap or a plate or saucer, and nuke on high for just 1 1/2 minutes. Uncover your snow peas as soon as the cooking time is up or they'll continue cooking and end up mushy!

Put the bagged greens in the bowl first. Now core your green pepper, dice it, and spread it on top of the lettuce. Slice your celery fairly thin, and make a layer of that. Take your half onion, slice it in half again, then slice paper thin. Make a layer of onion. The next layer will be your snow peas.

In a separate bowl, mix together the mayonnaise, sour cream, ranch dressing, and Splenda. Now make a layer of this, "frosting" the top of the salad with the dressing. Scatter the bacon evenly over the dressing, and the cheese over that. Chill your salad until dinner. To serve, scoop down through all the layers for each serving.

YIELD: 8 servings

Each serving will have 8 grams of carbohydrate and 2 grams of fiber, for a usable carb count of 6 grams; 3 grams protein.

☼ Asparagus Salad with Orange Vinaigrette

There's something about using asparagus in a salad that's just inherently elegant—and asparagus is one of the lowest-carb vegetables there is!

3 pounds (1.5 kilograms) asparagus

1/4 cup (60 milliliters) white wine vinegar

1/4 teaspoon orange extract

1 tablespoon Splenda

1 clove garlic

1 teaspoon gingerroot

1 teaspoon Dijon mustard

1/4 teaspoon dried tarragon

1/3 cup (80 milliliters) extra-virgin olive oil

First, snap the tough ends off the asparagus where they break naturally. Cut your asparagus on the diagonal into 1" (2.5-centimeter) lengths. Put the asparagus cuts into a microwavable casserole with a lid, add a couple of tablespoons of water, cover, and microwave on high for just 4 minutes. Uncover the asparagus as soon as it's done, or the steam will continue to cook it.

Whisk together everything else, pour it over the asparagus, and stir to coat. Chill for several hours, stirring now and then if you think of it.

YIELD: At least 10 servings

Each serving will have 4 grams of carbohydrate and 2 grams of fiber, for a usable carb count of 2 grams; 2 grams protein.

☀ Crunchy Snow Pea Salad

Different and good! Do use snow peas instead of sugar snap peas—they're lower carb.

    2 cups (150 grams) snow peas
    4 slices bacon
    1/3 cup (50 grams) roasted, salted cashews
    1 cup (160 grams) diced celery
    1 cup (150 grams) diced cauliflower (about 1/2" [1.25-centimeter] chunks)
    1/2 cup (120 milliliters) ranch salad dressing
    1/2 cup (120 grams) plain yogurt
    1 teaspoon spicy brown mustard

You'll want to pinch off the ends of your snow peas first, and pull off any tough strings. Cut them into 1/2" (1.25-centimeter) pieces. Put your bits of snow peas in a microwavable bowl, add a tablespoon or so of water, and cover with a saucer or with plastic wrap. Microwave on high for just 1 1/2–2 minutes, then remove from the microwave and uncover to stop the cooking.

Put the bacon on a microwave bacon rack or in a glass pie plate and microwave 4 minutes on high or until crisp, then drain.

While the bacon's cooking, coarsely chop your cashews. Combine all the vegetables, including the snow peas, in a mixing bowl. Combine the ranch dressing, yogurt, and mustard; pour over the vegetables and toss. Crumble in the bacon, add the cashews, and toss again. Chill before serving.

YIELD: 4–5 servings

Assuming 4, each will have 8 grams of carbohydrate and 2 grams of fiber, for a usable carb count of 6 grams; 5 grams of protein.

☀ Cucumber-Tomato Salad

Summery and refreshing, this salad is similar to those I've had at Middle Eastern restaurants. A natural with shish kebabs, but try it with anything!

1 medium cucumber, quartered lengthwise, then cut in 1/2"
   (1.25-centimeter) pieces

1/2 medium red onion, sliced paper thin

2 small tomatoes, cut in 1/2" (1.25-centimeter) cubes

1 cup (60 grams) chopped fresh parsley

1/2 cup (120 milliliters) olive oil

1/4 cup (60 milliliters) red wine vinegar

2 cloves garlic, crushed

Salt and pepper

Just put your cut-up vegetables and the parsley in a mixing bowl. Add the oil, vinegar, and garlic; salt and pepper to taste; and toss. That's it!

YIELD: 6 servings

Each serving will have 6 grams of carbohydrate and 1 gram of fiber, for a usable carb count of 5 grams; 1 gram protein; 254 milligrams of potassium!

☀ Spinach-Orange Salad

Wonderful with a simple steak or with grilled seafood.

 8 ounces (230 grams) triple-washed spinach or baby spinach

 1 navel orange

 1/4 medium red onion

 3 tablespoons extra-virgin olive oil

 2 tablespoons white wine vinegar

 1/8 teaspoon orange extract

 1/2 tablespoon Splenda

 1 teaspoon lemon juice

 1 1/2 teaspoons Dijon mustard

 Salt and pepper

Place your spinach in a salad bowl. Peel the orange, separate the segments, and cut each segment into three pieces—do all this over the spinach so that any juice that drips gets added to the salad. The bits of orange go in, too, of course! Slice the onion paper thin and put it in, too.

Pour the olive oil over the salad and toss until every millimeter of the spinach is gleaming. Now whisk together everything else, adding the salt and pepper to taste. Pour this over the salad, toss again, and serve immediately.

YIELD: 4 servings

Each serving will have 8 grams of carbohydrate and 2 grams of fiber, for a usable carb count of 6 grams; 2 grams protein.

☀ Bread and Butter Pickles

Bread and butter pickles are a favorite on burgers, as a barbecue side, and chopped up in deli salads. But like all sweet pickles, bread and butter pickles have plenty of sugar in them. So, I took some sour pickles—very low carb!—and added Splenda and the seasonings typical of bread and butter pickles. The result was delicious! I made these with pickle spears, since that's what form I could find plain sour pickles in, but if you find chips or whole pickles, feel free to use them instead.

> 1 24-ounce (680-gram) jar plain sour pickles (not dill, not garlic)
>
> 1/2 cup (120 milliliters) Splenda
>
> 1/4 teaspoon ground allspice
>
> 1/4 teaspoon celery seed
>
> 3/4 teaspoon dry mustard or 1 1/2 teaspoons whole mustard seed
>
> 1 pinch ground cloves
>
> 1/4 small onion

Pour the liquid off of the pickles, into a medium saucepan. Add the Splenda, allspice, celery seed, dry mustard or whole mustard seed, and cloves. Bring to a simmer, and let simmer for 3–4 minutes. While it's simmering, thinly slice the onion and add it to the jar. Pour the liquid over the pickles and onion, screw the lid on tight, and let the whole thing cool before refrigerating. These will be ready after a day or two in the fridge.

YIELD: About 16 spears

Each spear will have 2 grams of carbohydrate and 1 gram of fiber, for a usable carb count of 1 gram—but that includes all the liquid in the jar. If you don't drink pickle juice (and really, who does?), you can count on a lower carb count—I'd figure about 0.5 grams per spear. Only a trace of protein.

chapter ten

Festive Grillside Adult Beverages
(*Plus One for Everyone!*)

About Alcohol

Alcohol is a controversial subject in low-carb circles, and with good reason. You see, alcohol is one of the very few regularly consumed calorie-containing substances that doesn't fall into the category of protein, carbohydrate, or fat. Alcohol is, technically, a category unto itself, with 7 calories per gram.

However, of the three recognized macronutrients, alcohol has the most in common with carbohydrate, I'm afraid—not surprising, since alcohol comes from carbohydrate. Indeed, there are people who feel that alcohol should be counted with carbohydrate, gram for gram. If you feel you need to be this careful, be aware that the average drink—1 shot of 80-proof liquor, or 1 beer, or 1 glass of wine—contains roughly 14 grams of alcohol.

Not everyone feels that alcohol must be counted as a carb, however. Indeed, in the 1960s, there was a low-carb diet called The Drinking Man's Diet, a reference to the fact that, technically speaking, hard liquor contains no carbohydrate. I also have a low-carb book called *The Martini and Whipped Cream Diet*. And I myself have successfully lost weight on a low-carb diet that included a drink or two virtually every evening.

However, all discussion over whether alcohol is really a carbohydrate in disguise aside, three things are abundantly clear: First of all, alcohol is loaded with calories, something that we cannot entirely ignore. Second, alcohol will slow fat burning dramatically—or to use the phrase I once saw in a medical journal article, "Alcohol profoundly inhibits lipolysis." Be aware that the moment you start drinking, you stop burning fat until you've burned through all your alcohol calories. Indeed, if you drink and you're having trouble losing, alcohol is the most likely culprit. And third, alcohol, because it lowers inhibitions, can make you more vulnerable to the carb-loaded snack foods so often served with drinks—chips and such.

Still, for many of us, the idea of giving up all alcohol for life is daunting, and there is considerable evidence that moderate drinking is a strong protection against heart disease. Many of us—me included—will decide that we need to learn to manage our low-carb diets to allow for moderate drinking.

So, if you decide that a festive adult libation or two is going to be part of your cookout, you'll want to keep your consumption moderate, and you'll want to eliminate as many of the extra carb grams as you can. How to do this?

First of all, shun "alco-pops"—wine coolers, hard lemonade, Zima, and the like. These things invariably have a bunch of sugar added. Too, avoid all sugary mixers—not only cola, but most fruit juices and even tonic water. (There is diet tonic available; look for it.) Steer clear of liqueurs, as well—stuff like Midori, Kahlua, Bailey's Irish Cream, triple sec, and all the other syrupy, sugary alcohols out there. Sweet wines are also out, as is most beer.

What does this leave? Actually, quite a lot.

Beer

Beer is indisputably the number one adult beverage of choice at barbecues and cookouts. There are at least four widely available beers that will fit into our diet. Michelob Ultra is the lowest carb, at 2.8 grams per bottle. Just slightly higher are Miller Lite and Milwaukee's Best Light, both around 3.5 grams per 12-ounce (360-milliliter) can or bottle. If you'd like something a bit more robust, Amstel Light, at 5 grams a bottle, is the best-tasting beer I've tried that falls into the "really low carb" class.

Most of the rest of the "light" beers are too high carb for me to be able to recommend them—Bud Light is about 6.7 grams a can, and Michelob Light has 11 grams per bottle! Stick to the beers listed above, unless you've read the label and are sure that "light" means "low carb." New beers aimed at the low-carb market are coming out even as I write this, so our choices should expand very soon!

Beyond Beer

What if you're not a beer drinker, or want something different, or a little more festive? No problem! We've still got all the hard liquors to work with: vodka, gin, rum, tequila, whiskeys of all kinds, not to mention dry wines, which average 2–4 grams of carbohydrate per 5-ounce (150-milliliter) serving. Diet soda, diet tonic water, club soda, sparkling water, Crystal Light and other artificially sweetened fruit-flavored beverages, lemon and lime juice, and even the new low-sugar cranberry juice cocktail give us plenty of options! (Do not, however, use Rose's Lime Juice—it has added sugar. Use fresh or bottled unsweetened lime juice.)

Here are some ideas for refreshing summer drinks—and remember, no driving!

 Daiquiri

Forget all those strawberry daiquiris and banana daiquiris—this is the original, and it's remarkably refreshing.

> 1 shot lime juice
> 2 shots white rum
> 1 tablespoon Splenda

You can make this two ways: on the rocks or frozen. For a daiquiri on the rocks, simply mix all the ingredients well and pour over ice. For a frozen daiquiri, plunk all the ingredients, plus 3–4 ice cubes, in your blender, and blend till the ice is pulverized.

YIELD: 1 serving

4 grams of carbohydrate, no fiber, no protein (hah!).

☀ Mockahlua

This recipe originally appeared in *500 Low-Carb Recipes*, but since it's useful for mixing, I thought I'd better repeat it! This recipe makes quite a lot, but don't worry about that. Hundred-proof vodka's a darned good preservative; your Mockahlua will keep indefinitely.

    2 1/2 cups (600 milliliters) water

    3 cups (700 milliliters) Splenda

    3 tablespoons instant coffee crystals

    1 teaspoon vanilla

    1 bottle (750 milliliters) 100-proof vodka (use the cheap stuff)

In a large pitcher or measuring cup, combine the water, Splenda, coffee crystals, and vanilla. Stir until the coffee and Splenda are completely dissolved.

Pour the mixture through a funnel into a 1.5- or 2-liter bottle. (A clean 1.5-liter wine bottle works fine, so long as you've saved the cork.) Pour in the vodka. Cork, and shake well.

YIELD: 32 servings of 1 1/2 ounces each—a standard shot.

Each will have 2 grams of carbohydrate, no fiber, and the merest trace of protein.

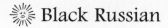 # Black Russian

    1 shot vodka

    1/2 shot Mockahlua

Just pour both liquors over ice in a rocks glass. That's it!

YIELD: 1 serving

2 grams of carbohydrate, no fiber, no protein.

 # White Russian

    1 shot vodka

    1/2 shot Mockahlua

    1 shot heavy cream

Combine, and pour over ice if desired.

YIELD: 1 serving

3 grams of carbohydrate, 0 grams fiber, 1 gram protein.

☀ Frozen White Russian

This is seriously decadent, and not as low carb as some of our other beverages—I'd recommend stopping at one! Still, this makes a great dessert for an adults-only cookout.

> 1 shot Mockahlua
> 1 shot vodka
> 1/2 cup (65 grams) sugar-free vanilla ice cream

Put everything in a blender, and run the blender until well combined. Pour into a smallish glass—a rocks glass or a wineglass will work nicely.

YIELD: 1 serving

The carb count on this will depend on the brand of sugar-free vanilla ice cream you use. If you use one of the lowest-carb—Atkins Endulge or Breyer's Carb Smart—your drink will have 6 grams of carbohydrate, 0 grams fiber, 3 grams protein. And will be unbelievably, decadently delicious.

☀ Gin Rickey

This old-fashioned cocktail is one of my new favorites!

> 1 tablespoon lime juice
> 1 shot gin
> Club soda to fill

Put the lime juice and gin in the bottom of a tall glass. Fill with ice, then add club soda to the top.

YIELD: 1 serving

1 gram of carbohydrate, a trace of fiber, and a trace of protein.

☀ Margarita Fizz

I included a recipe for Margarita Mix in *500 Low-Carb Recipes*, but because of the large amount of lemon and lime juice, not to mention Splenda, it was higher carb than we should drink on a regular basis. So I came up with this lighter alternative.

> 1 shot tequila
>
> 1 shot lime juice
>
> 1 1/2 teaspoons Splenda
>
> 8 ounces (240 milliliters) unsweetened orange-flavored sparkling water

Put the tequila, lime juice, and Splenda in the bottom of a tall glass, and stir. Fill with ice, and pour in orange-flavored sparkling water to fill.

YIELD: 1 serving

4 grams of carbohydrate, a trace of fiber, and a trace of protein.

☀ Seabreeze Sunrise

If you like fruity drinks, try this!

> 1 shot tequila
>
> 1 shot low-sugar cranberry juice cocktail (Ocean Spray makes one)
>
> 8 ounces (240 milliliters) pink grapefruit–flavored Crystal Light
>
> (or any no-sugar grapefruit-flavored drink mix)

Combine the tequila and cranberry juice cocktail in a tall glass, fill with ice, and pour in the grapefruit-flavored drink.

YIELD: 1 serving

3 grams of carbohydrate, 0 grams fiber, and 0 grams protein.

Hard Lemonade

Commercially made hard lemonade is actually a malt beverage—in the same class as beer. High carb right there, plus, of course, it has sugar. But how hard can it be to make your own?

> 1 shot vodka
>
> Sugar-free lemonade (both Country Time and Wyler's make a
>   sugar-free lemonade mix)

Just fill a tall glass with ice, pour in the vodka, and fill with sugar-free lemonade. Garnish with a lemon slice, if you like!

YIELD: 1 serving

1 gram carbohydrate, 0 grams fiber, and 0 grams protein.

Mojito

I'm tragically unhip. I discovered the Mojito while writing this book, and fell in love with it—only to learn it had been the hot drink for at least a year! If you haven't tried this classic Cuban drink, you must. (Don't have fresh mint? There's nothing easier to grow—indeed, plant mint and it will threaten to take over your yard!)

> 1 shot white rum
>
> 1 tablespoon lime juice
>
> 1 sprig fresh mint
>
> 1 teaspoon Splenda
>
> Club soda to fill

Combine the rum, lime juice, mint, and Splenda in the bottom of a tall glass. Using the back of a spoon, press the mint well to release the flavor, and stir everything together. Now fill the glass with ice, then with club soda.

YIELD: 1 serving

2 grams carbohydrate, a trace of fiber, and a trace of protein.

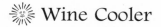 Wine Spritzer

This is a great drink if you want something mild that you can sip on for a while without getting, er, incapacitated.(A good thing to bear in mind if you have to play around with the grill rack and manipulate hot coals!)

> 3 ounces (90 milliliters) dry red wine
> Unsweetened berry-flavored sparkling water

Pour the wine over ice in a tall glass, and pour in berry-flavored sparkling water to fill.

YIELD: 1 serving

1 gram carbohydrate, 0 grams fiber, a trace of protein, and 61 calories.

Wine Cooler

You have a lot of leeway here! Basically, you're combining wine and diet soda. Experiment to find your favorite combinations.

> 3–5 ounces (90–150 milliliters) dry wine—red or white, whichever you prefer
> Diet soda—consider trying lemon-lime, red raspberry, tangerine or orange,
>   or grapefruit (Fresca)

Pour the wine over ice in a tall glass, and fill with the soda of your choice.

YIELD: 1 serving

Assuming you use 3 ounces of wine, this will have about 1 gram of carbohydrate, 0 grams fiber, and a trace of protein.

☀ Salty Dog

This old summer favorite is, of course, usually made with grapefruit juice—at 22 grams a cup. Better use the pink grapefruit–flavored Crystal Light!

> Coarse salt
>
> 1 shot gin
>
> Crystal Light pink grapefruit–flavored sugar-free drink mix
>
> (or any no-sugar grapefruit-flavored drink mix)

Rim a tall glass with salt. Fill it with ice, and add the gin and Crystal Light grapefruit-flavored drink.

YIELD: 1 serving

1 gram carbohydrate, 0 grams fiber, 0 grams protein.

☀ Dark and Stormy

A classic Dark and Stormy is made with ginger beer, not ginger ale, but there is no such thing as low-carb ginger beer, at least that I know of. So, I tried it with diet ginger ale, and got a very tasty drink!

> 1 shot dark rum
>
> 1 shot lime juice
>
> Vernor's Diet Ginger Ale (I like to use Vernor's because it's particularly crisp,
>
> but if you can't find it, use any diet ginger ale you can get.)

Put the rum and lime juice in a tall glass, add ice, and fill with ginger ale.

YIELD: 1 serving

3 grams of carbohydrate, a trace of fiber, and a trace of protein.

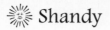 Shandy

This is a classic British summer cooler. If you make two, you'll use up all the beer and all the ginger ale!

> 6 ounces (180 milliliters) chilled light beer
>
> 6 ounces (180 milliliters) chilled diet ginger ale

Simply combine the two in a tall beer glass.

YIELD: 1 serving

Using the lowest-carb light beer, this will have less than 2 grams of carbohydrate per serving, with no fiber, and a trace of protein.

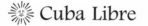 Cuba Libre

Bet most of you thought of this on your own, but for those of you who didn't . . .

> 1 shot white rum
>
> Diet cola
>
> Wedge of lime

Put the shot of rum in a tall glass, fill with ice, and pour diet cola to the top. Squeeze in a wedge of lime.

YIELD: 1 serving

2 grams of carbohydrate, a trace of fiber, and a trace of protein.

 # Sangria

A refreshing summer favorite!

> 1 1/2-liter bottle of dry red wine—burgundy, merlot, or the like
>   (You can use the cheap stuff!)
> 2/3 cup (160 milliliters) Splenda
> 1/2 teaspoon orange extract
> 1/2 teaspoon lemon extract
> 1 orange
> 1 lemon
> 1 lime
> Orange- or lemon-flavored unsweetened sparkling water

Pour the wine into a nonreactive bowl. Stir in the Splenda and the extracts.

Now, you have to decide if you're going to serve your sangria from a punch bowl or put it into a clean old jug. Me, I put it in an old 1-gallon vinegar jug, but then, I was taking my sangria camping.

If you're going to put your sangria in a punch bowl, simply scrub your fruit and slice it as thin as humanly possible. Put it in the punch bowl with the wine/Splenda mixture, and let the whole thing macerate for an hour or so before serving.

If you're using a jug, you'll need to cut your fruit into small hunks that will fit through the neck. Force the fruit into the jug, then pour the wine/Splenda mixture over it. Again, let it macerate for at least an hour.

When the time comes to serve your sangria, fill a tall glass with ice, pour in 4 ounces (120 milliliters) of the wine mixture, and fill to the top with lemon- or orange-flavored sparkling water.

YIELD: 12 servings

6 grams of carbohydrate (assuming you actually eat all the fruit, which you won't—I'm figuring it's really between 4 and 5 grams), a trace of fiber, and a trace of protein.

☀ Sweet Tea

This is the only nonalcoholic beverage in this chapter, but it's an important one! Sweet tea—iced tea with plenty of sugar in it—is the default summer beverage in the South. Here are the proportions for making a big pitcher of this classic, without the sugar.

> 6 cups (1.5 liters) water
>
> 4 family-sized tea bags
>
> 1 cup (225 milliliters) Splenda
>
> Water to fill

Bring the 6 cups of water to a boil in a saucepan, then add the tea bags. Let it simmer for just a minute, then remove from heat and let it sit for about 10 minutes. Remove the tea bags, squeezing them out in the process.

Add the Splenda, and stir briefly to dissolve. Now pour this concentrate into a gallon pitcher, and fill with water. Serve over ice!

YIELD: Makes 16 servings of 8 ounces each

3 grams of carbohydrate, a trace of fiber, a trace of protein.

Note: Want to make this virtually zero carb? Order some Zero Carb Syrup Base Concentrate—a concentrated liquid form of Splenda—from www.locarber.com. If you want a version with no artificial sweeteners, you can try using stevia; I know people who like stevia even better than sugar or Splenda in iced tea. I favor a blend of stevia extract and FOS (a naturally occurring long-chain sugar too big to be digested by the human gut) called Stevia Plus—look for it at health food stores. The label says 2 tablespoons equals 1 cup of sugar in sweetness, but I'd taste as you go.

chapter eleven

Desserts— If You've Still Got Room!

You know how it is—you've put back ribs, slaw, even a couple of beers. You're just as full as you can be. But it's a party, and you have that nagging feeling that something more is needed to complete the feast.

Here is a variety of delicious, sugar-free desserts to cap off your outdoor meal. You'll find that they range from light-on-both-carbs-and-calories ices and sherbets to rich and indulgent pies, cheesecakes, ice cream, and even real frozen custard. Personally, I'd pair the lighter desserts with the more filling main courses, like ribs, and the richer desserts with less-filling fare, like fish or poultry. That decision, however, is up to you!

☼ Margarita No-Bake Cheesecake

I saw Emeril make a margarita cheesecake on his show one night, and I had to decarb it the very next day! Fabulous. You can make this with cream cheese and sour cream, if you like, for added richness, or with Neufchatel cheese and plain yogurt for a lower calorie count with no increase in carbs.

> 1 1/2 tablespoons unflavored gelatin
>
> 1 cup (225 milliliters) Splenda
>
> 3/4 cup (180 milliliters) boiling water
>
> 1 1/2 pounds (680 grams) cream cheese or Neufchatel cheese, softened

1 cup (240 grams) sour cream or plain yogurt

1/4 cup (60 milliliters) lime juice

2 teaspoons grated lime rind

$1/2$ teaspoon orange extract

$1/4$ cup (60 milliliters) tequila

 Sweet-and-Salty Almond Crust (page 230)

Combine the gelatin and Splenda in a saucepan, and pour the boiling water over them. Stir over low heat until the gelatin is completely dissolved. Turn off the burner.

Put the softened cream cheese or Neufchatel cheese in a mixing bowl, and beat with an electric mixer until very soft and creamy. (If you have a stand mixer, you can start the cheese beating before you dissolve the gelatin, and just leave the mixer mixing on its own.) When the cheese is very smooth and creamy, add the sour cream or yogurt, and beat that in well, scraping down the sides of the bowl as needed. Next, beat in the lime juice, grated lime rind, orange extract, and tequila. Go back to your saucepan of gelatin. It should still be liquid! If it's not, you'll need to heat it again, gently. Beat the gelatin mixture into the cheese mixture and make sure everything is very well combined. Pour into the Sweet-and-Salty Almond Crust, and chill for at least 4 or 5 hours, and overnight is better.

Run a knife around the cake, between the cake and the rim of your springform pan, before removing the rim. Slice with a thin-bladed knife—dipping the knife in hot water before each slice is a good idea, although not essential.

Garnish with paper-thin slices of lime, strips of lime zest, or both.

YIELD: 12 servings

Each serving will have 11 grams of carbohydrate and 2 grams of fiber, for a usable carb count of 9 grams, and 12 grams of protein.

☀ Sweet-and-Salty Almond Crust

Emeril made his crust with crushed pretzels, to get that salty note so characteristic of margaritas. We're not going to use pretzels, of course, so I came up with this crust instead. It's great with the margarita-flavored filling!

1 1/2 cups (225 grams) almonds

1/3 cup (40 grams) vanilla whey protein powder

1/4 cup (60 milliliters) Splenda

1/4 cup (60 grams) butter, melted

1 tablespoon kosher salt (I like kosher salt for this because the larger grains make a real contribution)

Preheat oven to 325°F (170°C). Have on hand a 9" (23-centimeter) springform pan assembled and well sprayed with nonstick cooking spray.

Put your almonds in your food processor, with the S-blade in place. Run the food processor until the almonds are ground. Add the vanilla whey protein powder and Splenda, and pulse to mix. You may need to open the processor and run a knife around the bottom edge of the bowl, to get everything into the path of the blade. Now, turn the processor on and pour in the butter while it's running. Let everything blend—and once again, you may need to do the knife-around-the-bottom-edge-of-the-processor trick. When the butter is evenly distributed, turn off the processor. Add the kosher salt, and pulse the processor just enough to distribute the salt throughout the mixture.

Press firmly into the prepared pan, making sure you cover the seam around the bottom—but don't expect to be able to build it all the way up the sides or anything. Bake for about 10 minutes, or until lightly golden, and cool before filling.

YIELD: 12 servings

4 grams of carbohydrate, and 2 grams of fiber, for a usable carb count of 2 grams; 8 grams protein.

☀ Lime Cheesecake with Ginger Almond Crust

Using Neufchatel cheese in this cheesecake gives a lower calorie count without increasing the carb count, and still gives a superb flavor and texture.

16 ounces (450 grams) Neufchatel or cream cheese, softened

$^1/_2$ cup (120 milliliters) Splenda

2 eggs

$^1/_2$ cup (120 grams) plain yogurt or sour cream

Juice and grated rind of 1 lime

$^1/_2$ teaspoon vanilla extract

Ginger Almond Crust (page 232)

Preheat oven to 325°F (170°C).

With your electric mixer, beat the Neufchatel or cream cheese until smooth and fluffy. Beat in the Splenda, eggs, and yogurt, in that order, beating well after each addition. Scrape down the sides of the bowl often with a rubber scraper. Now, beat in the lime juice, rind, and vanilla extract. Pour into prepared crust. Put a flat container of water on the floor of the oven, then put your cheesecake on the oven shelf. Bake for about 45 minutes, or until only the very center of the cake jiggles a little when you shake it. Chill well before serving.

YIELD: 8–10 servings

Assuming 8, each will have 11 grams of carbohydrate, with 3 grams of fiber, for a usable carb count of 8 grams; 15 grams protein.

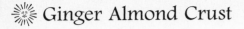 # Ginger Almond Crust

1 1/2 cups (225 grams) almonds

1/4 cup (30 grams) vanilla whey protein powder

1 teaspoon ground ginger

2 tablespoons Splenda

1/4 cup (60 grams) butter, melted

Preheat oven to 325°F (170°C).

Put your almonds in your food processor, with the S-blade in place. Run the processor until the almonds are ground medium-fine. Add the protein powder, ginger, and Splenda, and pulse to combine. Add the butter, and pulse to combine—you may need to run a knife around the bottom of the food processor to make sure everything gets combined.

Press firmly into a 10" (25-centimeter) pie plate or springform pan you've sprayed with nonstick cooking spray, building up the sides by about 1" (2.5 centimeter)—if you're using a springform, make sure you cover the seam at the bottom. Bake for 8–10 minutes or until it just barely turns golden.

YIELD: 8–10 servings

Assuming 8, each will have 5 grams of carbohydrate and 2 grams of fiber, for a usable carb count of 3 grams; 6 grams protein. These figures are included in the analysis for Lime Cheesecake with Ginger Almond Crust (page 231).

✺ Peanut Butter and Jelly Pie

I invented this for my peanut butter–obsessed husband, who adored it.

Jelly layer:

1 cup (120 grams) raspberries (fresh, or frozen with no sugar)

2 tablespoons water

3 tablespoons Splenda

Peanut butter layer:

1 package (4-serving size) sugar-free vanilla instant pudding mix

1 cup (225 milliliters) heavy cream

1 cup (225 milliliters) water

1 cup (225 grams) natural peanut butter

1/2 teaspoon blackstrap molasses

1/8 teaspoon salt

Cinnamon Almond Crust (page 234)

Put your raspberries, 2 tablespoons water, and Splenda in a saucepan over medium-low heat, and bring to a simmer. Stir until the berries are quite soft, and mash up with a fork. Turn off burner and set aside.

With an electric mixer, beat the pudding mix with the heavy cream and water until smooth and starting to thicken. Beat in peanut butter, molasses, and salt, scraping down the sides of the bowl as needed, until everything is well combined and very smooth.

Spread the raspberry mixture evenly over the bottom of the prepared Cinnamon Almond Crust. Spoon the peanut butter mixture evenly over the raspberry layer. Chill for at least several hours, and overnight is better.

YIELD: 8 servings

Each serving will have 16 grams of carbohydrate and 6 grams of fiber, for a usable carb count of 10 grams; 17 grams protein—which means you can legitimately have a slice for breakfast, if you want to.

Cinnamon Almond Crust

   1 1/2 cups (225 grams) almonds

   1/3 cup (40 grams) vanilla whey protein powder

   2 tablespoons Splenda

   1/2 teaspoon cinnamon

   1/4 cup (60 grams) butter, melted

Preheat oven to 325°F (170°C).

Put your almonds in a food processor with the S-blade in place. Run the food processor until the almonds are medium-fine. Add the protein powder, Splenda, and cinnamon, and pulse the processor to blend. Turn the processor on and pour in the butter—if needed, stop the food processor, run a knife around the bottom to make sure everything mixes evenly, put the lid back on, and process a little more.

Spray a 10" (25-centimeter) pie plate with nonstick cooking spray. Turn the almond mixture into the pie plate and press firmly and evenly into place, building it up the side by about 1" (2.5 centimeters). Bake for 8–10 minutes or until turning golden. Cool before filling.

YIELD: 8 servings

Each serving will have 6 grams carbohydrate and 3 grams fiber, for a usable carb count of 3 grams; and 8 grams protein. These figures are included in the analysis of the Peanut Butter and Jelly Pie (page 233).

☀ Peanut Butter Cup Pie

Easy! And who doesn't love chocolate and peanut butter?

> 1 package (4-serving size) sugar-free instant chocolate pudding mix
>
> 2 tablespoons unsweetened cocoa powder
>
> 1 cup (225 milliliters) heavy cream
>
> 1 cup (225 milliliters) water
>
> 3/4 cup (75 grams) natural peanut butter (I used creamy)
>
> 1 Simple Almond Crust (page 236)

In a large bowl, combine the pudding mix and cocoa powder. Pour in the heavy cream and water, and beat with an electric mixer to combine well. Then beat in the peanut butter until everything's well combined. Pour mixture into cooled crust, scraping it all out of the bowl with a rubber scraper. Spread evenly in crust, and chill.

YIELD: 8 servings

Each serving will have 12 grams of carbohydrate and 4 grams of fiber, for a usable carb count of 8 grams; 14 grams of protein.

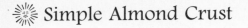 Simple Almond Crust

1 1/2 cups (225 grams) almonds

1/4 cup (30 grams) vanilla whey protein powder

1/4 cup (60 grams) butter, melted

Preheat oven to 350°F (180°C).

Using your food processor with the S-blade in place, grind your almonds to a consistency similar to cornmeal. Add the protein powder and butter; pulse to combine well. Turn out into a pie plate you've sprayed with nonstick cooking spray, and press firmly and evenly into place, building up around sides. Bake for 12–15 minutes or until edges are starting to brown lightly. Remove from oven and cool.

YIELD: 8 servings

Each serving will have 6 grams of carbohydrate and 3 grams of fiber, for a usable carb count of 3 grams; 7 grams protein. This analysis is included in the figures for the Peanut Butter Cup Pie (page 235).

Tin Roof Freezer Pie

This started out with Cocoa-Peanut Logs, a simple cookie-bar recipe in *500 Low-Carb Recipes*, and just—grew!

Crust:

3 ounces (85 grams) sugar-free dark (semisweet) chocolate
    (2 average-sized bars)

1/4 cup (60 grams) natural peanut butter

2 cups (60 grams) crisp soy cereal (like Rice Krispies, only made
    from soy—Keto makes one)

Filling:

2 packages (4-serving size) sugar-free vanilla instant pudding mix

1 cup (225 milliliters) heavy cream

1 cup (225 milliliters) water

2 cups (260 grams) no-sugar-added vanilla ice cream, softened (but not melted!)

1 batch Sugar-Free Chocolate Sauce (page 245)

1/2 cup (75 grams) dry roasted, salted peanuts, chopped

Over lowest possible heat, melt the sugar-free dark chocolate and the peanut butter together. Mix them up, then stir in the crisp soy cereal, stirring until the cereal is evenly coated with the chocolate/peanut butter mixture. Turn this mixture into a 10" (25-centimeter) pie plate you've sprayed well with nonstick cooking spray, and press firmly into place. Chill your crust while you make the filling.

In a good-sized mixing bowl, combine the pudding mix, cream, and water, and beat with an electric mixer until well combined. Add the softened ice cream, and beat until just combined.

Pour half this mixture into the now-chilled chocolate–peanut butter crust, and top with half the chocolate sauce. Pour in the rest of the filling, top with the rest of the sauce, and sprinkle the chopped peanuts on top.

Stash your pie in the freezer, and chill it for at least several hours. Then take it out of the freezer about 15–20 minutes before you plan to serve it, to let it soften a bit, but not thaw, before you serve it.

YIELD: 8–12 servings

Assuming 8, each will have 8 grams of carbohydrate and 3 grams of fiber, for a usable carb count of 5 grams; 13 grams protein.

☼ Mud Pie

Frozen coffee pie with a chocolate crust and chocolate sauce! What's not to like? This has a mild coffee flavor, but feel free to add more instant coffee granules—tasting as you go—if you like it more intense. Also feel free to use decaf if you, like me, have trouble sleeping if you have caffeine after dinner!

  2 packages (4-serving size) sugar-free vanilla instant pudding mix

  1 cup (225 milliliters) water

  1 cup (225 milliliters) heavy cream

  3 tablespoons instant coffee crystals

  2 cups (260 grams) sugar-free vanilla ice cream, softened (but not melted!)

  Chocolate Cookie Crust (page 239)

  1 batch Sugar-Free Chocolate Sauce (page 245)

Put your pudding mix, water, and heavy cream in a good-sized mixing bowl, and beat them with your electric mixer until they're well blended. Beat in the coffee crystals, then the softened ice cream. Beat just long enough to get everything mixed together; then pour half of the filling into your prepared Chocolate Cookie Crust. Top with half of the chocolate sauce. Add the rest of the filling, and top with the remainder of the sauce.

Stash your pie in the freezer for at least several hours. Then take it out a good 15–20 minutes before you serve it, to let it soften a bit (but not thaw!).

YIELD: 12 servings (I know that sounds like a lot, but I've tried serving bigger slices, and people get too full!)

Each serving will have 9 grams of carbohydrate and 3 grams of fiber, for a usable carb count of 6 grams.

 Chocolate Cookie Crust

   1 1/2 cups (225 grams) almonds

   5 tablespoons butter, melted

   1/3 cup (40 grams) vanilla whey protein powder

   1/4 cup (60 milliliters) Splenda

   1/4 cup (30 grams) unsweetened cocoa powder

   2 tablespoons water

Preheat oven to 325°F (170°C).

Put the almonds in your food processor with the S-blade in place. Run the processor until the almonds are finely ground. Add the butter, vanilla whey protein powder, Splenda, and cocoa, and pulse the food processor until everything is well mixed. Add the water, and pulse until you have a soft, sort of sticky mass.

Turn this into a 10" (25-centimeter) pie plate you've sprayed well with nonstick cooking spray, and press evenly into place, building all the way up the sides. Bake for 7–10 minutes or until set. Cool before filling.

YIELD: 12 servings

Each serving will have 5 grams of carbohydrate and 3 grams of fiber, for a usable carb count of 2 grams; 6 grams protein.

☀ Lime~Honeydew~Ginger Ice

Light, refreshing, and brilliant green.

> 1 package (4-serving size) sugar-free lime gelatin
>
> 2 cups (480 milliliters) boiling water
>
> 2 cups (320 grams) honeydew melon, cubed
>
> 1 1/2 tablespoons grated gingerroot
>
> Juice and grated rind of 1 lime

Assuming that you have a blender that can deal with boiling water, put the gelatin and the boiling water in your blender, and whirl until the gelatin is completely dissolved. If your blender won't take the heat, whisk the water and the gelatin together in a bowl, instead, until the gelatin is completely dissolved. Let it cool to a temperature your blender can take, before you do the next step.

If you've used a bowl to dissolve your gelatin, pour it into the blender now, turn it on, and add the honeydew, a few chunks at a time. When the honeydew is all pureed, add the gingerroot and lime juice, let it whirl another couple of seconds, and then turn off the blender.

Put your blender container in the fridge, and chill until it's starting to thicken up. Pour it into an ice cream freezer, and follow the directions for your model, until the granita is frozen; then serve. Or you can do this in traditional granita form, which is to freeze it in a shallow pan and scrape it with a fork every 20–30 minutes as it freezes to separate the crystals.

You can just pour this into dessert cups and let it chill as a gelatin dessert instead, if you prefer.

YIELD: 8 servings

Each serving will have 4 grams of carb, a trace of fiber, and a trace of protein.

☀ Peach Ice Cream

This isn't dirt-low in carbs, but it's astonishingly delicious, with a fabulous, creamy texture. If you make only one frozen dessert from this book, make this one.

16 ounces (480 milliliters) peach-flavored Fruit$_2$O

1 tablespoon unflavored gelatin

2 cups (400 grams) sliced peaches (unsweetened frozen peach slices work great)

1/4 cup (60 milliliters) lemon juice

1/3 cup (80 milliliters) Splenda

2 cups (480 milliliters) heavy cream, chilled

3 tablespoons sugar-free vanilla pudding mix

Pour the Fruit$_2$O into a nonreactive saucepan, and turn the burner underneath to medium-low. Sprinkle the gelatin over the top. Stir with a whisk as the mixture heats, making sure all the gelatin dissolves.

Add the peaches, lemon juice, and Splenda to the gelatin mixture, and simmer for about 10 minutes or until the peaches are just getting tender. Transfer the mixture to your blender (this assumes your blender can take the heat—if it can't, let the mixture cool a bit first) and pulse the blender a few times—you want to leave some small chunks of peach, rather than pureeing everything completely smooth.

Let the peach mixture cool until it's room temperature—it should be syrupy, but not gelled, when you get to the next step, which is:

Pour your chilled heavy cream into a large mixing bowl, and add the pudding mix. Whip with an electric mixer until the cream stands in soft peaks. Turn the mixer to low, and beat in the peach/gelatin mixture. Beat only long enough to get everything blended, then turn off the mixer.

Pour the whole thing into your ice cream freezer. (This actually was a bit too much mixture for my freezer, so we had to eat the little bit left over unfrozen. This was not a hardship.) Freeze according to the directions that come with your freezer, then serve.

If you have leftover Peach Ice Cream, let it soften at room temperature for at least 15 minutes before serving—it's likely to be unappealingly hard straight out of the freezer.

YIELD: Makes about 1 1/2 quarts, or roughly 10 servings, assuming you're using self-restraint, which is actually a bad bet.

Assuming you manage to share, and not pig out, each serving will have about 10 grams of carbohydrate, with 1 gram of fiber, for a usable carb count of 9 grams; 2 grams protein.

☼ Vanilla Frozen Custard

Rich and delicious! The polyols in this help to keep it from freezing like a rock—which it would if you used Splenda instead. Try serving it with the Sugar-Free Chocolate Sauce (page 245).

> 6 eggs
> 2 cups (480 milliliters) half-and-half
> 1/2 cup (100 grams) granular polyol sweetener
> 3 tablespoons sugar-free imitation honey
> 1/4 teaspoon salt
> 2 cups (480 milliliters) whipping cream, chilled
> 1 tablespoon vanilla extract

In a medium saucepan, beat together eggs, half-and-half, sweetener, honey, and salt. Cook over low heat, stirring constantly (don't quit or you'll get very rich scrambled eggs!), until mixture is thick enough to coat a metal spoon and has reached at least 160°F (75°C).

Cool quickly by setting pan in ice or cold water and stirring until it's just barely warm—this prevents trapped steam from making your custard watery. Cover and refrigerate until thoroughly chilled, at least 1 hour.

When you're ready to freeze your custard, whip your cream with the vanilla, using an electric mixer until it stands in soft peaks. Turn the mixer to low and beat in the custard, running the mixer just enough longer to blend well. Pour the mixture into your ice cream freezer, and freeze according to the directions that came with your freezer; then serve.

YIELD: Makes between 1 1/2 and 2 quarts, or 10 servings, at least!

Assuming 10 servings, each will have 8 grams of carbohydrate, not counting polyols; 6 grams protein.

☀ Lime-Vanilla Sherbet

In Ray Bradbury's extraordinary novel *Dandelion Wine*, the characters, visiting an ice cream parlor, choose the unusual flavor "Lime-Vanilla Ice." Consider this my tribute to one of the greatest American novels of the twentieth century.

> 1 package (4-serving size) sugar-free lime gelatin
>
> 2 cups (450 milliliters) boiling water
>
> Juice and grated rind of 1 lime
>
> 5 tablespoons Splenda
>
> 2 cups (480 grams) plain yogurt
>
> 1/4 cup (30 grams) vanilla whey protein powder
>
> 2 teaspoons vanilla extract

If your blender can take the heat, combine the gelatin and boiling water in your blender container, and whir to dissolve the gelatin. If your blender can't take the heat, stir the two together in a heatproof container until the gelatin is completely dissolved, then let the mixture cool to the point where your blender can handle it (but the whole thing is still liquid) and pour it into your blender container. Put it on the blender base, and turn it on to a low speed. Add the other ingredients, one at a time, adding the yogurt in several additions to avoid overwhelming your blender.

When everything's well blended, let the whole thing cool until it's starting to get really syrupy. Pour into your ice cream freezer, and freeze according to the directions for your unit.

YIELD: 8 servings

Each serving will have 5 grams of carbohydrate, a trace of fiber, and 5 grams of protein.

 Orange Sherbet

Isn't orange everybody's favorite flavor of sherbet?

> 1 packet sugar-free orange gelatin
>
> 2 cups (480 milliliters) boiling water
>
> 2 cups (480 grams) plain yogurt
>
> 5 tablespoons Splenda
>
> 1/4 cup (30 grams) vanilla whey protein powder
>
> 2 tablespoons lemon juice
>
> Juice and grated rind of 1 orange

If your blender can take the heat, combine the gelatin and boiling water in your blender container, and whir to dissolve the gelatin. If your blender can't take the heat, stir the two together in a heatproof container until the gelatin is completely dissolved, then let the mixture cool to the point where your blender can handle it (but the whole thing is still liquid) and pour it into your blender container. Put it on the blender base, and turn it on to a low speed. Add the other ingredients, one at a time, adding the yogurt in several additions to avoid overwhelming your blender.

When everything's well blended, let the whole thing cool until it's starting to get really syrupy. Pour into your ice cream freezer, and freeze according to the directions for your unit.

YIELD: 8 servings

Each serving will have 5 grams of carbohydrate, a trace of fiber, and 5 grams protein.

☀ Sugar-Free Chocolate Sauce

This is as good as any sugar-based chocolate sauce you've ever had, if I do say so myself. Which I do. Wonderful over the Vanilla Frozen Custard (page 242) or over store-bought no-sugar-added ice cream, for that matter, and essential for the two freezer pies in this chapter. Don't try to make this with Splenda, it won't work—the polyol sweetener somehow makes the water and the chocolate combine. It's chemistry, or magic, or some darned thing.

1/3 cup (80 milliliters) water

2 ounces (60 grams) unsweetened baking chocolate

1/2 cup maltitol

3 tablespoons butter

1/4 teaspoon vanilla

Put the water and bitter chocolate in a glass measuring cup, and microwave on high for 1–1 1/2 minutes or until chocolate is melted. Stir in the maltitol and microwave on high for another 3 minutes, stirring halfway through. Stir in the butter and vanilla, and it's ready to serve (or make into a pie!).

Note: This worked beautifully with maltitol. However, when I tried to make it with erythritol, it started out fine but crystallized and turned grainy as it cooled—though it would still have been okay used hot over ice cream, it wouldn't have worked for the frozen pies in this chapter.

YIELD: Makes roughly 1 cup, or 8 servings of 2 tablespoons each.

2 grams of carbohydrate and 1 gram of fiber, not including the maltitol, for a usable carb count of 1 gram; 1 gram protein.

Where to Find a Few Less-Common Ingredients

Sugar-Free Imitation Honey

HoneyTree brand imitation honey is available from the HoneyTree Company:

> HoneyTree, Inc.
> 8570 Monroe Rd., Onsted, MI 49265
> Phone: (517) 467-2482

At this writing, the minimum order is 12 bottles, but that will set you back only $22, not too bad, and it'll keep. Consider getting a group of low-carbing friends together to share an order!

At this writing, Carb Smart is also planning to carry HoneyTree Sugar Free Imitation Honey: http://www.carbsmart.com.

Steel's brand of imitation honey is available from:

> **Synergy Diet:** http://www.synergydiet.com
> **Low Carb Outfitters:** http://www.lowcarboutfitters.com

I've had readers report that they've found sugar-free imitation honey at Wal-Mart!

Polyols

DiabetiSweet (isomalt blended with the artificial sweetener acesulfame-K) is available through:

> http://www.puritans.com
>> (This is also where I buy most of my vitamins.)
>
> http://www.diabeticproducts.com
> http://www.focuspharmacy.com
> http://www.diabetesstore.com

And, according to some of my contacts, it's also available at some Wal-Mart stores! It's generally worth looking at any pharmacy in the diabetic-supplies section. This makes DiabetiSweet the easiest polyol sweetener to obtain.

Erythritol is available through:

> http://www.carbsmart.com
> http://www.lowcarbgrocery.com
> http://www.lowcarbnexus.com

(**Note:** Erythritol didn't work out for the chocolate sauce recipe in this book, so if that's what you want to make, go for maltitol or DiabetiSweet instead.)

Maltitol is available through

> http://www.carbsmart.com
> http://www.lowcarbnexus.com

Xylitol is available through

> http://www.synergydiet.com

(**Note:** I have no personal experience cooking with xylitol.)

Liquid Splenda

As long-time low carbers are aware, the big drawback of granular Splenda is the maltodextrin used to bulk it to the same sweetness-per-cup as sugar. This makes granular Splenda very easy to use, but it also gives it 24 grams of carbohydrate per cup—far, far less than sugar, but enough to give one pause. Liquid Splenda, being "bulked" with water, doesn't have this problem. However, McNeil, the company that makes Splenda, has steadfastly refused to make liquid Splenda available to the American public.

At this writing, I know of two sources of what amounts to liquid Splenda, being sold as "syrup base." Here they are:

Zero Carb Syrup Base Concentrate is sold by http://www.locarber.com. An 8-ounce bottle will run you $17.99 plus shipping. That sounds steep, but since it's very concentrated—4 drops replace 1 teaspoon of granular Splenda—it's actually cheaper to use.

I actually obtained some of the Zero Carb Syrup Base Concentrate after I had finished developing recipes for this book. It strikes me as a very useful product, and I will be developing recipes with it in the future. If you'd like to substitute it for the granular Splenda in these recipes, there is a conversion chart on the back of the bottle. It gives the equivalent quantities of Syrup Base to sugar—figure it's the same for Syrup Base to granular Splenda, since granular Splenda measures one-for-one with sugar.

Nature's Flavors (http://www.naturesflavors.com) carries a "low carb sweet base" and a "low carb acidic base," which are basically liquid Splenda with a little flavor added. These run $8.49 a quart; however, these are much more dilute than the Zero Carb Syrup Base Concentrate, which makes them more expensive to use. Also, they add liquid to your recipe, which you'll need to compensate for.